THE VIOLIN

THE VIOLIN.

HOW TO MASTER IT.

By

A Professional Player

(WILLIAM CRAWFORD HONEYMAN)

GYAN

Published by

Gyan Publishing House
5, Ansari Road
Daryaganj, New Delhi-110002
Phone: 011-47034999, 9811692060
E-mail: books@gyanbooks.com

Distribution Network
gyanbooks.com
India, USA, Canada, UK, Australia

ISBN: 978-93-6208-338-8 (HB)
First Published, 1883

2nd Impression 2024

Printed at: Gyan Press, Delhi.

THE VIOLIN
Author: A PROFESSIONAL PLAYER (WILLIAM CRAWFORD HONEYMAN)

THE

VIOLIN.

HOW TO MASTER IT.

By

A Professional Player.

Boston:
Published by Jean White,
226 Washington Street.

PREFACE.

WHILE there are "Violin Tutors" and "Schools" filled with music and exercises in abundance, no work devoted simply to the practical exposition of the difficulties of the instrument and their mastery has ever been written or published. Hundreds living far from any teacher struggle blindly with these difficulties, contracting habits fatal to success, and never to be shaken off; and hundreds more are wilfully allowed to remain in ignorance by dishonest or incompetent teachers, anxious only for long-continued fees. Those and all lovers of the instrument this work is intended to assist. In these chapters the struggling students have clearly and lucidly mapped out for them a course by following which they may correctly teach themselves; while even adepts, or those within reach of good tuition, will find much information that is fresh and of great practical value for their guidance and advancement in this delightful study.

With a view to making the work complete in every particular, and anticipating as far as possible the many questions which will be put by intelligent students concerning points not ordinarily treated in instruction-books, an appendix of hints, advice, and suggestions has been added to its other welcome features, which will be found very useful. The publisher hesitates not to recommend the work as "the most comprehensive, the most precise, most perspicuous, and withal the least costly book in violin-playing ever issued."

BOSTON, 1883.

CONTENTS.

THE VIOLIN:

HOW TO MASTER IT.

CHAPTER I.

THE POWERS OF THE VIOLIN.

NO instrument ever has been, or ever will be, I suspect, invented capable of even approaching the violin in extraordinary power and variety of expression. Its vocal singing; its smooth sliding; the impassioned power of a sweep from one end of the string to the other; its weird *tremola;* its pensive and velvety *legato;* its clear, birdlike harmonics; its pearly staccato bow; its wailing chords; the mellow *vox humana* of its bass string; the flutelike sweetness of its third; and the ringing brilliance of its upper register, can scarcely be excelled even by the human voice. All other instruments give but a clumsy imitation: this all but outrivals the thing imitated. Hear the overtures of "Semiramide" or "William Tell" imitated on a piano-forte or organ,—for even under the fingers of a master it can be but an imitation; observe how all the short notes are either buried in a mass of groaning harmony, or never attempted to be fingered; then hear the same compositions rendered by a full orchestra, every note, however short, standing out sharp and clear, and then understand in part what makes the violin monarch of every musical instrument. Again, hear a piece of dance-music, no matter of what nationality, executed by a flute or piano-forte, and afterwards listen to the same piece performed on the violin. The first is as a theatrical scene, all scumbling and coarse daubing, compared with the clearness and minute beauty of a picture by Raphael. The shortest note, in the faintest whisper or most noisy *fortissimo*, the most rapid run or the swiftest chromatics, can be executed with a precision and perfection attainable on no other instrument. In another and more scientific sense the violin is the only perfect instrument. A piano cannot be tuned perfectly, and the flute that will play in tune on all its keys has never yet been made. Where these and other instruments stagger and limp, the violin springs to the front without an effort. Volumes might be written on its majestic powers, but what good? The violin reached perfection two hundred years ago,—for, except in the setting back of the neck a little to increase the pressure of the strings, on account of our heightened concert pitch, and give greater command of the high notes, and a slight thickening of the bass bar, no alteration of importance has been made on the Cremona models,—and at the same time became king of all. Its reign is undisputed, and therefore needs no demonstration.

SELF-TUITION POSSIBLE.

The question is often asked by ardent lovers of the violin, Is it possible to learn to play it without a teacher? I have no hesitation in answering, that, with steady application, quickness, and observation, it is. But, just as a person may learn to read French by the aid of books alone, but must hear the language spoken before a complete mastery is acquired, so the student of the violin must at least *see* good players performing. With hundreds it is impossible to get near a competent teacher; but even these may at intervals see a good performer, watch the style of fingering, the straight sweep of the bow, the graceful bend of the fingers of the right hand, the position of the instrument, the wrist, and the fingers, and the apparently marvellous manner in which the left hand may fly up and down the string with perfect precision. All these things must be seen to be understood: how they are accomplished it shall be my endeavor to explain. This proviso understood, the proper books being studied, and the proper amount of *hard work* being given, there is no reason why a student should not teach himself. The spring and incentive to all knowledge must come from within. All that a teacher can do is to indicate how the same difficulties have already been mastered, and prevent the formation of bad habits. Whether *all* teachers do so is quite another question. Teachers are not all competent, and, even when competent, are not all honest. They must live, poor souls! Their bread depends on their pupils continuing as long as possible to place fees in their hands; and one can hardly blame them for dealing out the precious knowledge in homœopathic doses.

THE PERNICIOUS TEACHER.

Then, again, there is what I may call the pernicious teacher, — the man who has formed a theory of his own in regard to the position of the instrument or the handling of the bow; the man to whom all the great masters, such as Spohr, Baillot, David, Campagnoli, Kreutzer, Loder, Blagrove, and the rest, are as nobody; and who deforms his pupils for life by drilling them into his own style, till they may actually be picked out without prompting in a crowd. A student is better without teaching at all than with lessons from such a master. One such blind leader of the blind I have in my mind's eye, whose peculiar cat's-paw-like style of holding the bow I caronceognize at a glance in any pupil who has had the misfortnoted study under him. One of these pupils I met a year or two ago, fifty miles from the town in which this teacher lives, noted the position at once, and said curiously, "Who taught you?" and then was not at all surprised to hear named the teacher I have described. Another teacher I have before me — a lady this time — who holds her bow about two inches from the nut, as if these two inches of hair were a superfluous encumbrance; and a third who thinks nothing of expending an hour of the pupil's time in teaching him to rosin his bow, and who *always* wastes at least half of the hour in "blathering" about himself and the feats he has done. Another I remember whose bow described a half-moon curve in crossing the strings; and how such a player could turn out a pupil with flexible wrist, I am at a loss to understand.

THE CHOICE OF A TEACHER.

My own advice to the student is to be sparing in the *number* of lessons he takes, but to be certain that they are taken from a teacher with a position in the musical world, and one having that unmistakable grace of style by which a good player may be picked out by a deaf man. All that is technical I shall endeavor to put practically before him, giving, in so doing, the hard-won experience of a lifetime. Steady application and unremitting toil, with such observation and help as I have indicated, must do the rest.

THE ROYAL ROAD TO LEARNING.

A few dollars expended on a thorough and conscientious teacher may do much; but, after all, the student must rely almost solely upon himself. The royal road to learning is *hard work.* When this is accompanied by enthusiasm, the results are so wonderful that it is often misnamed genius.

MUSICAL NOTATION.

The first step towards mastering the violin is the learning of musical rotation, just as the first step to book-lore is the study of letters and syllables; but as there is nothing, however simple, which may not be made to appear difficult, this very trifling task has been made a sore bugbear to many a distracted beginner. A knowledge of the elements of harmony is a simple matter; yet there is no book on harmony published, that I am aware of, that would not make even a professional musician's hair almost stand on end with its frightful terms and incomprehensible lessonsions. A good practical knowledge of the old notation may easacquired in two lessons. I never had to give more to any pupil, and will here lay down the process by which the task is made easy.

DEFECTS OF THE SOL-FA NOTATION.

A young pupil once came to ask me in great concern, and asked if it was possible to play the violin by the tonic sol-fa notation. That was the only notation he understood; and, like hundreds more, he was staggered by the *look* of the other,—strongly averse to attempting to master it. My answer was not given either in haste or ignorance, as I understood both notations; but it was given decidedly against the sol-fa as *instrumental music.* Any one can understand how, when we look at a long word in ordinary typography, such as Constantinople, we do not spell the syllables out in letters like a child. Familiarity with the syllables has taught the eye to group them at a glance into one phrase. In like manner, in

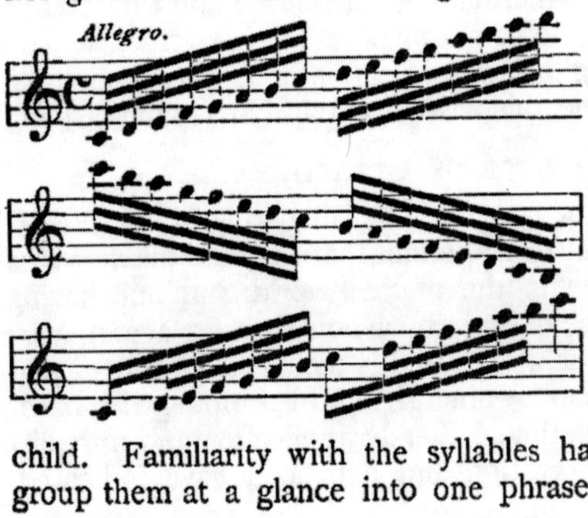

reading *at sight* a rapid passage in music, such as the foregoing, it is impossible to read every note by name. There is not time for that. The reader can only make a dash at it, glancing at the first in the phrase, and then hastily following the form or outline of the notes on the stave to the last, thus getting a *picture* of the music on the mind, and, while executing it, may be busily photographing what follows. That is impossible with the sol-fa notation. The letters representing the notes run on in an even line, and cannot be grouped even into syllables. They must be read singly and separately, therefore slowly; they speak to the mind more than to the eye; they cannot be read mechanically. For this reason the sol-fa notation must be condemned unflinchingly as instrumental music.

HOW TO MASTER THE OLD NOTATION IN TWO LESSONS.

That was the substance of my answer to the pupil I have alluded to; but at the same time I undertook to prove to him practically that, for instrumental music, the old notation could be learned in a shorter time than the sol-fa. I lines is purpose I drew five lines on a blank sheet of paper, — and the student who wishes to follow me may do the same, — then placed the G clef at the beginning, with two ledger lines above and two below the stave. I then wrote the names of the notes G, A, B, C, etc., on their respective lines or spaces, from G on the fourth string to D on the first. I then took the violin in my hand, and showed him that the four strings were named G, D, A, and E, and the place where these were found on the stave. This gave him an intelligible *anchorage* for his ideas. I then showed him how the intervening notes were got by stopping the strings with the first, second, and third fingers; and then, to give him a firmer hold of the new study, I showed him how the notes on the five lines and spaces, when read from the top downwards, gave the words FED and BAG, and the spaces when read upwards gave the word FACE. "Now," I added, "sit down for half an hour, and learn off by rote, as you would a school-task, the names of these notes and the lines or spaces they fall on, so as to be able to tell me the name of the note, and how it is got on the violin the moment I point to it on the stave." I then left him, and in less than the allotted time the difficulty was mastered. I then drew on the same sheet of paper a round ○ lying on its side, representing a semibreve, explained the value of it in time; then cut it into two minims; explained how they each represented half the value of the first; divided these into four crotchets; explained again; then into quavers and semiquavers. This done, he had mastered common time. I then gave him triple time, and explained how to accent the two, illustrating this last by lines of poetry in both rhythms; showed how sharps and flats at the signature affected the keys; and the task was over. I gave him the paper for home study; but practically the whole theory was mastered in these two short lessons. Any one may do so as easily for himself. At the beginning of every Violin Tutor the elements of the notation are given, generally with a diagram of the finger-board of the violin, such as I will give in a subsequent chapter, to show where the notes are to be found; and by following the simple process above described, and then following out the more minute details at leisure, an intelligent grasp of the notation may be gained in a few hours which will last for a lifetime.

OLD AND NEW NOTATIONS CONTRASTED.

The great stronghold of simplicity in the old notation, so far, at least, as instumental music is concerned, is that there is no movable set of syllables representing the scale, and changing with every key. C always falls on the same lines or spaces; and so would the other letters, no matter how many sharps or flats may constitute the signature. Then in violin music another element of difficulty is removed in the fact that only one clef is used. In concluding this chapter, then, I would strongly advise the student to abandon silly prejudice, and boldly attack the old notation at once, assured that all its dreaded difficulties will vanish at a glance. Sol-faists are bitterly prejudiced against the old notation; and, noting the incalculable blessings it has brought to us in making music popular and intelligible with the youngest, they rashly conclude that it is the only perfect system, and that all others are doomed. Those who understand only the old notation, again, are as lofty in their scorn of the meaningless-looking stuff which is shown them as music, and plainly hint that none but maniacs would dream of comparing the two. Alas, they are both right, and they are both wrong! for there are advantages in knowing both, which only they can realize who have mastered the two. For mere instrumental music, however, nothing more simple, nothing better than the old notation, has ever been devised; and nothing as perfect for all kinds of music exists.

CHAPTER II.

THE BOOKS TO USE, AND WHERE TO GET THEM.

A LONG road, which happens to have so many windings in it that its length is not seen at a glance, never appears so wearisome as one that is straight. Mastering the violin is travelling a long, and at times trying, road; but, if the stages are so judiciously planned that the whole of the difficulties to be surmounted do not appear at once, the task not only becomes easy, but a continued and fascinating pleasure. This thought I throw out in passing on to the choice of a Violin Tutor.

SPOHR'S "VIOLIN SCHOOL."

It is true that no violin school has ever been given to the world so masterly, and so calculated to foster a pure and classical style, as Spohr's "Violin School;" but this is not a book for a beginner. It begins with the simplest elements of music and instructions, certainly; but, as it embraces the whole range of violin-playing, it is like setting a young traveller to face a long, straight road to put this in his hands. In addition to this, the studies are so severe, so absolutely painful in many cases to perform, that the book tends to chill rather than excite ardor. The student begins to shirk his lessons: the great book is gradually neglected, and often finds its way to the obscurity of some dusty shelf, where after a while may be found also the violin and bow with which such a promising start was made. Still another objection I might advance to the early use of this noble work. Spohr was so rigidly classical—pure and cold as a marble statue—that he could not descend to waiving a point, and remorselessly begins his pupils with the natural key, C. This necessitates the pupil playing the F natural on the first string, a most difficult feat for a beginner, and in my own experience thoroughly pernicious at that stage, when the hand is not fairly set to the position. There is a tendency to shift the hand to get the F in tune; or, if this be not done, the F is almost invariably played a slight degree sharp. The result is one of two things, — the hand acquires a shifty, uncertain movement, or the pupil contracts the fatal habit of playing not strictly in tune. All this may be avoided by temporizing a little, if I may so speak, by letting strict musical knowledge stand for the time in abeyance, and beginning with the three sharp keys, G, D, and A. If the relative minors of these are included (necessitating the playing of the sharp seventh of these keys, — that is, D sharp, A sharp, and E sharp, — which will be done at first by drawing back the finger), the ability to form the slightly flatter F natural will follow without difficulty. The hand, by the time these keys are mastered, will be tolerably well set to the instrument, and less liable to contract that chronic stiffness which ruins many a player for life.

DANCLA'S "VIOLIN SCHOOL."

As a *first* book or primer, however, I know of no better work than Dancla's "Violin School," published by Jean White, Boston, Mass. This tutor is simple and plain, and progresses easily, with scales and exercises.

HENNING'S "VIOLIN TUTOR."

Another excellent book, which may be used by beginners with benefit as an exercise book, is Henning's "First Book for the Violin," price one dollar, published by Jean White, Boston, Mass. This book contains some good duets, and many daily exercises after the style of Czerny's Five-Finger Exercises for the Piano-forte, calculated to set the hand and fingers. If the student has a teacher, six months ought to suffice for the study of Dancla; after which De Beriot or Alard may be attacked. De Beriot or Alard, like Spohr, are books for a lifetime, and may always be returned to even by the professional musician with pleasure.

"MASTERY" A RELATIVE TERM.

The student who has followed me thus far may begin to get frightened, and say to himself, "I could never master the violin: I need not dream of it." Or he may say, "It is clear that to master this instrument requires the study of a lifetime: it must be the student's sole occupation. I have not time for that; I had better try some easier instrument."

Now, in one sense this is sound, and in another it is utterly fallacious. The "mastery" of an instrument at best is but a relative term. We cannot all be Joachims or Nerudas, and even they are always learning; but, however poorly we may play, there is no reason why we should not play in the proper manner. It is as easy—actually easier in reality—to play upon the violin with the instrument in its proper place and position, with the bow held freely and gracefully, and the body erect and at ease, as with the dozens of bad habits with which ignorance or indifference fetter their victims for life. To all, therefore, I would say, Begin right; keep right in the method of your playing, and then advance as far as you can in that direction. This is all that the poorest player or the most gifted genius can accomplish; and, if the fruits are sometimes slower to appear, sweet are they when culled. Studied thus, the accomplishment is a never-ending source of delight. There are no limits to the execution, but those of your time and manipulative skill. The instrument, to begin with, is boundless in its resources; and at every fresh advance new effects and fresh beauties are unfolded to lighten the toil, and cheer the student on his way.

THE VIOLIN A LADY'S INSTRUMENT.

Again, I would say, there is no instrument more suited than this to a lady's hands. All that is feminine is required for its mastery,—tenderness, lightness, grace, swiftness, and dexterity. For this reason I unhesitatingly pronounce the violin *the* instrument of the future for ladies.

THE VIOLIN AND PIANO-FORTE CONTRASTED.

The piano-forte at best is but a vulgar, noisy, unreal, hard, and unsympathetic imitation of the harp; and, had it not been that it is almost as easy of mastery as a wire-strung dulcimer played with two sticks,—a mere question of execution and mechanical practice,—would never have attained the evil popularity it enjoys. It is soulless, and thoroughly unsatisfying. It excites our wonder; never moves our heart. It is brilliant and metallic,—transient as the love of a heartless woman, and showy and false as the glare and tinsel of a theatrical transformation scene. Yet, if any one has daughters, the question never seems to arise, "What instrument shall we set them to study?" It is taken for granted that there is but one instrument for a young lady,—the piano-forte; and to that they are drilled as soon as their little fingers can stretch a fifth. The violin—so pre-eminently suitable for them above all others; so full of soul and sweetness, and every kind of weird power that is to be found in music; so fitted for the display of every grace of arm, wrist, or body—is never thought of. All this must change, and the violin step forward to its proper place as the leading instrument for either sex. I rejoice to notice that the truth of what I have here laid down is yearly becoming more known and understood; and the spectacle of a young lady carrying her violin-case and music along the street, or playing in an orchestra, is so common as to be no longer the subject of rude staring or wondering remark. Where there are more daughters in a family than can get conveniently to the piano-forte for practice, it is becoming no uncommon thing for the outsider to be set to the violin, when, as a matter of course, this majestic instrument, when combined with the piano-forte, at once steps into its place as monarch of all by lending some of its soul to the inferior instrument. Let this go on and increase, and music—one of the chief sweeteners of existence—will receive a marvellous impetus in development. And, if the violin has its difficulties compared with the piano-forte, it has also its advantages. The music for it is all written in one clef; and the student has only one stave to read instead of two,—a difficulty of the piano-forte which some distracted young ladies never surmount. Not so often is the mistake made of setting boys to the piano-forte, unless they show such a defective "ear" as to make the mastery of the violin a hopeless task.

THE AGE AT WHICH TO BEGIN.

Given a sharp "ear," however,—that subtle ability to detect unerringly a false note in its minutest shades,—boyhood or girlhood is the time to begin the study of the violin with every hope of success. From eight to twelve, or even later in some cases, the muscles are soft, the joints loose and flexible, and the body unset. There need be no disguising the fact,—the left shoulder, arm, wrist, and collar-bone have to be *set* to the instrument, and the right arm, shoulder, elbow, and wrist have to be gradually adapted to the proper management of the bow, as surely and imperatively as the muscles of a professional acrobat have to be set in youth to the accomplishments of his feats. A pupil above eighteen or twenty before beginning, I never knew to make great attainments in the study. Even beginning at these ages I have seen very fair success; but it is far too late to give the instrument a fair trial, and many difficulties are then greatly increased by the joints having become set, and the muscles hard. Fifteen is quite late enough, as eight is just early enough; but a great deal depends upon the build of the pupil. In beginning early, however, care must be taken that the young pupils are not kept too closely at the instrument. The study ought to be gradual, so as not to dwarf the chest, with plenty of cricket or other out-door exercise to relieve it; just enough, indeed, to set the muscles and frame, and excite an interest and love of the instrument in the young breast. A smaller instrument and a shorter bow must be used, so that the pupil may not describe a curve with his bow in attempting to draw it the full length across the string.

CHAPTER III.

THE CHOICE OF AN INSTRUMENT.—GENUINE CREMONAS.

IN no case do we find such extraordinary and artificial prices given for instruments as for violins, as much as five thousand dollars being freely offered, and in some cases refused, for instruments by the best of the Cremona makers, which were eagerly sold by their makers for the modest sum of six florins. These are the best instruments in existence, both in regard to the wood of which they are made, the mellowness of age which they have acquired, the amber varnish with which they are coated, and the artistic excellence of their build and make; but he is a lucky musician, indeed, who can get hold of even a fair specimen of these wonderful instruments. The Cremona violins *were not all good;* and many that were have been hopelessly injured by being scraped, broken, patched, or "improved" by ignorant or fraudulent makers. Let the violin-player get that into his head lucidly and clearly to begin with, and he may be saved from disappointment even if a genuine instrument of the kind should come in his way. But such as were good, and have survived uninjured to our day, partake so much of the nature of rare antiquities that they are nearly all—more's the pity and crying shame—in the hands of persons who never use them, who will hand them down to their descendants, and keep them hugged and guarded till they crumble voiceless and mute into dust. There is something wrong there; but it is difficult to see how it could be remedied, unless some of these wealthy connoisseurs should see the error of their ways, and *lend for life* the instruments they possess to the different soloists of eminence, who, alas! are too often forced to discourse most eloquent music from poor copies. This would be a boon to the world, a benefit to the instruments,—for a good violin is greatly improved in tone by being constantly played upon in all the positions and on all the strings by a good player,—and no loss to the donors, as the violins would return to them on the decease of the player. This suggestion seems somewhat Quixotic, I admit; but it is not nearly so outrageous as that these gems of instruments should lie rotting in disuse.

CREMONA COPIES.

Putting aside the possession of a good Cremona as an all but impossible stroke of fortune, the pupil may turn to the copies of these instruments with some hopefulness and even satisfaction. I have played upon a genuine Cremona with real amber varnish, and a warranty of pedigree beyond suspicion, and for which a thousand dollars had been cheerfully paid, but which was so miserably thin and feeble in tone that I would have thought it dear at ten dollars; and, on the other hand, I have played upon a copy of a Stradiuarius by M. Vuillaume of Paris, that seemed as good to me as a Cremona, except the mere mellowness imparted by age. These copies are made from the well-seasoned pine taken from old Swiss *chalets*, are scrupulously exact reproductions of the Cremona models, and are covered with an imitation (by no means successful) of the old amber varnish. Like every thing else of genuine merit, however, the Vuillaume copies are themselves being copied, and the imitations being furnished with fraudulent Vuillaume tickets, so that the only guaranty a buyer can have is to order direct from the firm, or through one of their agents. In selecting a copy the novice should always get the aid of a professional player, who, for a small fee, or perhaps for the pleasure of the thing, will select an *improvable* instrument; that is, one with a quality and quantity of wood, and volume and quality of tone, which, through constant playing, will mellow or "rub down" into a good instrument. A violin, I may say, never gets *louder* in tone, however long it may be kept. But the quality of the tone so alters that, under certain circumstances, it might be thought to have increased in volume. This difference is chiefly in the *carrying* power of the tone. An old violin, when good, rings out in a large or even a heated hall, and actually appears louder in tone the farther you are from it; a new instrument is noisy and loud near the player, but stifled and poor in tone at a distance. A great deal of the tone producible from a violin, however, depends upon the power of the player. I have heard a masterly player perform a solo upon a wretched German instrument, — one of the Leipsic moulded fiddles, as they are called, — softening all its horrible hardness with a smooth bow and glassy fingering, making its very noisiness a beauty, and its shrillness the clearest and most ringing brilliance. "Dear me," said a pupil once to me, "my poor old fiddle sounds just as well in your hands as your own." He was mistaken, of course; but there was a deal of truth in the remark. How best to educe a good tone I shall show farther on. Let the possessor of a poor instrument, therefore, not repine and sigh enviously after genuine Cremonas with their deep, blood-red amber varnish and faultless symmetry, but remember that more than half the victory must come tingling from his own fingers. To put a real Cremona, indeed, into the hands of a learner would be a positive sacrilege, as it requires a master to do these noble instruments any thing approaching to justice.

GERMAN "CREMONAS."

In every music-store will be found a class of instruments ranging in price from two to about twenty dollars, and known to dealers and professional players as Leipsic fiddles. They are generally boldly ticketed as "Cremonas," and may be recognized at a glance by their thick, lumpy varnish, generally scraped off at the corners to give an appearance of age; their harsh and horrible tone, and a kind of sooty appearance given to the breastplate, or belly, about the hollows of the *ff* holes. These violins, I am told, are made by a quick and easy process, the wood being planed *flat* to the required thickness; then cut out in grosses to the form, as a confectioner cuts out peppermint lozenges; then put into a vat, and boiled into softness; and afterwards taken out, and put between moulds under tremendous pressure. The result of this violent treatment is, (1) that the wood is only artificially seasoned; (2) the fibres are violently warped out of their original lines, and can never vibrate freely; and (3) the instrument cannot improve as would one cut out and made in the proper manner. These violins are noisy and brazen in their deceptiveness, like every thing false. In a hot room they get sticky and stifled in tone, and all but dumb after a few hours playing in a steamy atmosphere. They are almost always stumpy and unwieldy in tone on the shift, particularly upon the third and fourth strings; they never answer readily to the bow, and in quick passages give forth, instead of a brilliant succession of neat notes, a mere confused scuffle of sounds. Beginners at the violin, however, are so often forced to study economy that a high-priced instrument is beyond their reach. I may therefore say that a German fiddle costing from ten to twenty dollars is quite good enough for a *first* instrument.

HOME-MADE VIOLINS.—A TRICKY MAKER.

In choosing an instrument *for life*,—and that need not be done till the student has been some time at the study of the instrument, and is capable of appreciating in some degree the power and tone of a good violin,—avoid these Leipsic or German fiddles rigidly. First be certain that it is a made, not a moulded, violin. Then be sure that it is not a violin merely made up by some needy person "to sell." One such character I have in my mind's eye, who has acquired a certain facility in rattling up instruments out of poor wood, and with hardly any tools. The violins he turns out are nice-looking instruments, of a pale-yellow color, and generally built on the model of a heavy, deep Stradiuarius. His mode of selling them is to pawn the instrument, and then get his wife, who goes about selling tins, to dispose of the ticket for a good sum to some unwary player. The violins thus forced into the market are horribly rasping in tone, generally false on some of the strings, and utterly beyond improving.

TESTING A VIOLIN.

The student should early accustom himself to note the appearance of all kinds of instruments, the curving of the *ff* holes, the varnish with which they are covered, and, above all, the tone they produce on every string and in every position. A good violin should be equal on every string, and free and responsive on the shift. A common fault is that the violin has a dreadfully loud and noisy fourth string, and a feeble and thin-toned third; or they may be good on the first and second, and thin and shallow-toned on the third and fourth. If the note G on the third string is good and full, the violin will generally be equal on all the strings. B♭ on the second string, and A♯ on the third, are generally poor notes, no matter how good or valuable the violin. Only an experienced player can test and select a good instrument. He alone can play on every string and position; he alone knows how to search for and unerringly detect faults on the various strings; and he alone has an ear so trained to varieties and qualities of tone as to be an authority upon which the novice may rely more safely and implicitly than upon the dealer, who is generally more ignorant in this respect than the merest tyro of a buyer.

Although an impostor in violin-making crops up here and there, there are dozens of good and reliable makers at home and abroad.

AMBER VARNISH.

There are dozens of recipes for making amber varnish; the simplest being to melt the amber in one vessel, and heat common turpentine in another, and suddenly mix them at a certain temperature. Davidson gives several recipes, and mentions naphtha, which is a native of Italy, as a good solvent for a fine amber varnish. I once spoke to an eminent dealer, who informed me that he was often called upon, or written to, by men professing to have discovered the ancient amber varnish; but, after seeing their specimens, he was strongly of opinion that at least part of the secret is lost. It seems to me, judging from that on my own violin and others which I have inspected, that with amber varnish the coating lies like a glassy but mellow and elastic skin on the top of the wood, while spirit varnish is absorbed deep into the pores, and so acts as a damper or clog upon the free vibration of the fibres. The tone imparted by spirit varnish is always hard, wiry, or unsympathetic; that of amber varnish, soft and mellow. Next, then, to having a well-made violin, is to have a properly varnished one. Mr. W. R. Mainds believes that he has discovered the real oil varnish used by the Cremona makers, which he thus describes: "The color is, when thinly spread, golden, and as it increases in thickness it becomes deeper, until it is blood-red, and beautifully transparent. I have put a violin of my own varnishing alongside some of the finest Cremonas in this country, and the color is identical, while the tone is full, round, and mellow." In a communication to me on the subject, Mr. Mainds says, "There is such a thing as the amber of commerce; but that is not amber, although extensively used in varnish-making. Amber proper is a gum of some extinct plant, which, from associating long with minerals, has become so altered or petrified, that its original nature is completely changed. The materials I use for my varnish belong to Italy, and would work much better there than in our cold climate. I have tried many experiments to make the much-talked-of amber varnish. I have employed many chemists, who readily undertook to dissolve amber. I have consulted makers of varnish, and, after all, am now prepared to say that amber, after having been fused, is useless for varnish-making, and, when dissolved by other means, does not give a sufficient percentage to furnish a body which will compare in any way with the varnish used by the Cremona makers. Their chief study was the making of the violin. Their varnish was a simple one, and that it was no secret is clearly proved by its having been used by them all. Sometimes their varnish is poor-looking, and in many cases seems to have been carelessly put on; but there is no doubt of its being an oil varnish, but that its gum is amber is doubtful."

From this statement it may be inferred that Mr. Mainds does not call his mixture an amber varnish. A specimen now submitted to me confirms in part his original description. The varnish, however, is poor in lustre, and certainly not so transparent or so rich-hued as one I am about to describe by another discoverer. The color, indeed, does not appear to be a liquid part of the varnish, but merely some gradual color which has been stirred into it, as it shows in minute red specks throughout the coating. There is good testimony, however, as to its improving the tone of violins covered with it; and it is undoubtedly an oil, not a spirit, varnish. Dr. George Dickson of Edinburgh (some of whose rich-toned instruments, made by himself, and exquisitely finished, I have seen) has discovered a varnish, which, if it is not the real Cremona one, is as like it in color, transparency, and characteristic tone as any I have seen. The color is a deep red, as if the white maple upon which it is laid were transformed into a rich-hued piece of mahogany. There are no minute spots of color discernible. Varnish and color appear to be one and indivisible; and, when the wood is sloped to an angle of thirty or thirty-five degrees from the spectator, it shows on every light veining of the wood a peculiarly beautiful golden sheen, or bronzed reflection. It is also transparent as some of the ancient deep-hued stained glass: it seems, indeed, to lie like a skin of that glass upon the surface of the wood.

NEW VIOLINS AS SOLO INSTRUMENTS.

A new violin, however well made, is almost useless as a solo instrument. The tone is generally loose and woody; the violin does not respond readily enough in rapid runs, *arpeggios*, or the staccato bow. It does not carry far, and in a heated hall appears thin and weak a few yards from the platform. Not being "set" with age, it also goes much more quickly out of tune. The Vuillaume violins are therefore noticed as suitable chiefly for orchestral playing, in which the finer qualities of tone are not so imperatively demanded. A hundred years hence, when they have acquired the rare qualities which only age can impart, they may command attention even as solo instruments.

THE WOOD OF VIOLINS.

Even more important than having a violin covered with the Cremona varnish is having the instrument made of well-seasoned, well-chosen wood, cut at that season when there is least sap in the tree. In this the Cremona makers excelled. A writer lately asserted, that, if the wood of the breast were only selected coarse in fibre,—that is, open in the grain,—the violin would be sure to be sonorous and ringing in tone; but the statement is contradicted by experience, and by many of the best of the real Cremonas, which are sometimes close in the grain, sometimes open, and sometimes fine in the centre, at the join, and coarser towards the sides. The wood ought to be *naturally* seasoned, and not forced by being boiled or steamed, or dried in an oven or a warm chamber; that is, it ought to lie for four or five years roughly blocked out in a dry, cool place. The wood sold in pieces in the music-stores ready for making violins is generally *forced* wood, therefore to be avoided. That, however, is a particular almost beyond the ken of the player, unless he actually supply the wood with which his violin is to be made, and one in which he must depend to a great extent upon the honesty and skill of the maker.

THE QUALITIES OF A GOOD VIOLIN.

To sum up, therefore: A violin is to be valued (1) by its artistic make; (2) its age and consequent mellowness of tone; (3) its equality of tone on every string and position; (4) the selection of the wood and the varnish with which it is covered; and (5) by the manner in which it has been preserved, played upon, and developed in tone by its different possessors.

In choosing a violin for life, any price from twenty to one hundred dollars may be given, though I may remark that it is not usual for parents to show much liberality in this particular. No good cottage piano-forte can be got for less than two hundred dollars. Parents know this, and give that sum, or more, freely; but when it comes to paying for a violin, which, if properly made, improves and increases in value, instead of deteriorating steadily like the piano-forte, they hesitate, and look grave over twenty or thirty dollars. It is one of the anomalies of life; and I attempt no explanation, and make no comment.

THE CHOICE OF A BOW.

The value of a good violin bow lies chiefly in the spring; that is, the curve downwards of the stick towards the hair. Five to ten dollars may be given for a bow good in appearance: yet in a year or two the spring leaves it, and it is quite worthless; while a good one may be hit upon by chance for five dollars, which stands long years of hard work without showing a sign of getting straight. For this reason a second-hand bow is better than a new one. If it be deficient, the fault will be seen. When the pupil is of age to use a full-length bow, whether the bow be selected new or old, he ought to choose one by a good maker, — Tourté, Dodd, Vuillaume, Tubbs, or any one having a reputation to lose, — and then select one suited in weight to his hand and taste. Some like a heavy and some a light bow; but, as each of these qualities is an advantage in certain kinds of playing, I think a medium weight is best.

TESTING A BOW.

In choosing the bow, first look along the top of the stick with the eye close to the nut, and see that it is perfectly straight; that is, not curved to the side, as well as towards the hair. Then screw it up till the bow is almost straight, — much tighter than it is required for playing, — and again look along the top of the stick. Not one bow in ten will stand this test without warping to one side, especially close to the point where the wood is thinner. If it remain even, unscrew it till the wood touches the hair, and look if the most prominent part the curve in the stick falls exactly in the centre of the hair. If it does, it is worth buying; and you can only trust to good fortune that it will stand the test of years. Even humanity does not always do that: so it is not surprising that a bit of curved wood should at times fail. A new bow has generally some silvered thread wound round the stick near the nut to keep the fingers from slipping on the smooth polished wood. When this is worn off, it should be replaced by a layer of thin glove leather, neatly glued on, so as to show no joins or corners. This leather substitute is a great ease and comfort to the thumb of the right hand.

THE HAIR OF THE BOW.

The hair of the bow must be always slackened immediately after playing, and at intervals taken out and renewed, — and that not merely when it is broken and worn to about half its proper width. Each hair, if looked at through a microscope, will be found to be serrated, — to have a number of minute spikes running in one direction. These spikes are an important factor in the drawing out of a good tone; and for this reason one-half — that is, about sixty — of the hairs should be put upside down, so that both up and down bows may get their fair share of spikes. After the hair has been used for a length of time, even though not one should be broken, the spikes get worn off. The hair, rosin as you may, refuses to grip firmly; and a crisp, clear note is an impossibility.

TO RE-HAIR A BOW.

Every player who is particular as to the tone he produces ought to re-hair his own bow, unless he can discover a patient, conscientious artist who will do it properly for him. The hair should be that of horses, which is whiter, less greasy, and more durable than that of mares. Place this hank in a dish of clean water, and then remove the old hair by forcing off the ferule of the nut with a penknife, being careful to preserve the little wedge which tightens the hair under the ferule, and also that which is found inside the box of the nut. Remove the other end of the hair by taking out the wedge in the point of the bow; then fix into the cavity the tied end of the new hank of hair, which is now wet through; tie up the point of the bow to a nail or gas-bracket; slip the ferule on to the hair; and then, with a clean, small tooth-comb, comb it out evenly, gripping the hair between the forefingers behind the comb, so that none of the hairs cross each other, or are of unequal tightness. Gauge then the length of hair required to reach the nut, and then clasp the flat band of hair close to this, temporarily, with an American spring music-clip, which may be bought for a penny, and to the faces of which have been glued two thin, flat pieces of wood. Tie the hair outside of this clip strongly with a double linen thread, burning the ends of the hair with a heated iron to cause the points to swell. Then turn the bow, stick upwards; insert the tied end of the hair backwards in the nut-box, fix the wedge, reverse the hair, slip in the slide-lid of the nut-box; bring down the ferule, lying loosely on the hair, to its place on the nut; spread the hair as widely and evenly as the ferule will allow, tap in the wedge, and replace the nut in the bow; then leave the hair slackly screwed till the morning, when it will be found tight, even, and dry, and ready for use. A bow should never, on any account, be re-haired with dry hair. A good stick might be warped, and for ever spoiled by such treatment.

ROSINING THE BOW.

In rosining the bow the hair should be drawn but three or four times back and forwards evenly across the surface, with a steady, firm pressure, and not too fast. Haste fires the rosin; while a gentle treatment brings it off crisp and white as flour. When the bow has been re-haired, powdered rosin, fine as flour, must be rubbed well into the hair from both sides as soon as it is thoroughly dry. The best rosin to use is a matter of taste. I find that the common rosin, if selected clear and light in color, gives a more crisp tone than any of the prepared cakes, and does not, like them, clog or dirty the hair. It is scarcely so fine for solo playing, but is much to be preferred for general use. The fingers must never touch that part used to rosin the bow; and the rosin should be put away in a box as soon as used, to guard it from grease and dust. In handling a bow the same precaution should be used; the fingers never touching the hair, except, as I shall show in the chapter on bowing, where the back of the thumb presses against it near the nut.

THE VIOLIN-CASE.

The bow ought to be kept in a case, fastened flat against the lid, and not in a bag, which greases the hair, wears it smooth, and tends to warp the stick. The case containing the violin and bow, and stock of strings, should be kept in a dry, cool place, neither warm nor cold, and not on the floor or close to a wall, or near any heavy curtains or articles likely to attract or retain dampness.

CHAPTER IV.

STRINGING THE VIOLIN.

EVERY thing about the study of the violin, to be done well, must be done with neatness and exactitude. Stringing the instrument is a simple operation; but there is nevertheless a right and a wrong way. The thickness of string best suited to the student's instrument can be decided only by experiment; but it is a safe rule to have the strings rather thin than thick. A thin string responds more readily; gives a purer tone; carries farther, though to the player it may seem weaker; and is sweeter in chords, and more brilliant and velvety high up on the shifts. Every student ought to keep a string-gauge, which may be had for a trifle in any music-store, and, having decided the size which best suits his violin and his taste, adhere to that most rigidly, being specially particular to have the different strings carefully graduated in size, so that the pressure on the breast of the violin may be such as to produce the greatest possible equality of tone, as well as perfect accord in the "stepping," or fingering. The most common error is to have a thick third string, under the mistaken impression that it gives more tone. The fourth ought always to be a silver-covered string, and not one of the dull, stumpy-toned copper-covered kind commonly used. A good silver fourth will last, with care, from one to three years: so the difference in price need not weigh heavily with the buyer; besides which, the silver-covered string has the peculiarity of imparting to the other strings much of its own brilliance and fluty resonance.

SEASONING STRINGS.

It is recommended by some that the strings should be occasionally rubbed with a flannel cloth saturated with almond oil; but I do not approve of an oiled string under any circumstances, my experience being that the drier a string can be made, without forcing it or actually beginning to decay, the better will be its tone, and the greater its durability. A string, indeed, can be "seasoned" just as judiciously as a piece of wood by being kept for months wrapped in paper, and enclosed in a tin box in a dry, cool place. Strings seasoned thus may be kept for a year and longer, and give out a more ringing and brilliant tone than those fresh from the maker. I give that as my own opinion, and the result of experience. Spohr says, "As gut-strings spoil when kept long, it is better not to buy more of them at a time than will be required in from four to six months;" but he gives no indication as to how long these strings are supposed to be in the dealer's hands before they are bought. The student had better experiment, and decide for himself. About the month of September is a good time to buy in a stock of strings, as they ought then to be "new-season" strings, fresh from the makers. It may be said that the fourth string, if not oiled occasionally, is apt to shrink in its covering, and give out a rattling sound; but that, I think, is more proof of a badly made string than of any need of oiling. An exceptionally good first string is often found in a bundle; and this, after using one length, may be put away, and kept for special occasions.

ITALIAN STRINGS.

Before stringing his violin, the student must buy the strings, and in doing so will find three different kinds claiming his attention. First is the ordinary gut-string; the best being made from the intestines of the skinny mountain sheep of Italy, and called Neapolitan, Roman, Verona, or Padua strings, according to the seat of their manufacture. For tone, brilliant yet pure, ringing yet delicate; for ready response to the lightest touch of the bow; and for trueness in the "stepping," or fingering, and sweetness in the harmonics, nothing has been found to approach these. The only question is one of durability, so many villanous substitutes are palmed upon the unwary student as "real Italians," which prove rotten, or false and unreliable, that he soon becomes disgusted; and again, when a real Italian or a good imitation is got, it is generally used raw from the maker, instead of being seasoned into toughness, or, still worse, has been rotted with oil, or kept so long or so carelessly, that it has begun to decay, and the result is still unsatisfactory. Again, in a very warm room, or a steamy atmosphere, or with a player inclined to perspire about the fingers, even a seasoned Italian string cannot be always depended upon; but, as the latter are altogether exceptional conditions, there is still a large majority of players, including myself, who cling to the use of the gut-string.

PERSPIRING FINGERS.

The player whose hands perspire heavily is truly to be pitied. Rubbing the hand and fingers over with a sponge dipped in spirits, or a little sugar of lead or milk, applied at night before going to bed, may modify the evil; and I have recommended, and found some to be benefited by, playing steadily at severe exercises with the violin in the proper position for as long as the arm will support the fatigue, — say, half an hour at a time, — not taking down the instrument even to turn over the leaves of the music. This seems to act as a kind of toughener to the fingers of the left hand. The sap appears to recede from the hand, and the fingers to become less plump and glossy with moisture.

SILK STRINGS.

Next to gut-strings fall to be noticed the acribelles, or silk strings, generally used only for the first. The good qualities of this string may be summed up in great durability in a warm room or steamy atmosphere, or with a player whose hand perspires. The tone is thin and wiry, and less sympathetic than that of a gut-string; and, the pressure being less on the bridge, the fingering is slightly different. This diminished pressure also affects the tone of the other strings injuriously, just as a good silver fourth affects the others advantageously. If the string be selected thick, it will increase the pressure somewhat; but, humor the silk string as you may, it can never compare in tone with that of a good gut, and is much more difficult to tune, the least touch at the peg sending it up half a tone.

STEEL STRINGS.

Next to silk strings naturally falls to be noticed the new string of silver and steel, called the "combination," an Amercan invention. This string is advertised as superior in tone to the finest Roman. It is not superior; it is inferior. From a specimen submitted to me for notice by a dealer, which I have tested on my own violin, I have made the following observations: (1) The sound of the string is metallic: it lacks the velvety softness of the gut-string; and it is always objectionable to have strings of a different quality on a violin. The difference in running from one to the other is offensive to the ear. (2) The sound of the open string is decidedly bad; but it improves steadily as you ascend till, from C upwards, it seems clearer than a gut, but somewhat ear-piercing in quality. Harmonics come out very clearly, but the natural ones are not in tune. The harmonic E in the centre of the string is a quarter of a tone flat (and the violin upon which I have made the test has the peculiarity of but rarely being false with a gut-string); and the harmonic E an octave above that, at either end of the string, is a semitone flat. This is a serious objection, apart from the difference in fingering of the ordinary notes, as you cannot modify the pitch of natural harmonics with the fingers, but must take them as they come. The harmonics, too, have also the ear-piercing quality of tone instead of the fluty softness of the gut. (3) The string has a disagreeable echo, and seems to vibrate in a sneaking way, even when only the other strings are being played upon. (4) The tone is clear and brilliant only with a strongly pressed bow. With a light bow, using only half of the hair, or playing a piano run or staccato bow, it fails to give either a good note or a ready response. I have a suspicion, from this fact, that the string will prove heavy on the hair of the bow, and wear it smooth in a very short time. (5) It is exceedingly difficult to tune. The wire is already strained to its utmost, and does not yield even so much as a silk string, which may be *tugged* into tune when the peg refuses to adjust the difference. From these facts I conclude that the silver combination string is not suitable for solo playing of the purest order, not for orchestral playing of the higher kind, in the midst of which one has very often to tune the first string by a mere speculative touch at the peg; but for playing in a hot ball-room, for the rougher kinds of work generally, or for an amateur who studies economy alone, who seldom uses harmonics, and whose ear is not yet sensible of the finer differences of tone, the string may do very well. It is said to last for many months; but I cannot speak on that point, as I removed the string after two-days' testing. I may add, that, the moment a good Italian gut-string was substituted, the other three strings acquired a more ringing, resonant, and fluty quality of tone, as well as greater volume of sound, thus indicating that the metal first string, like the silk, acts injuriously on the tone of the other three.

ADJUSTING THE BRIDGE.

Having chosen the strings, the student may now proceed to adjust them. The best height and width and thickness of the bridge can be decided only by experiment. A thick bridge with broad feet gives a stronger body of tone; a thin bridge tends to shrillness. A high bridge, by increasing the pressure of the strings, gives a louder tone; but the quality is not so good. French players, and those who love to indulge in much *tremola*, or close shake-playing, and a loud quality of tone, delight in a high bridge and nut; while those who prefer a smooth, sweet quality of tone, and ease and exactness in stepping the upper notes, generally adopt a lower bridge.

The bridge ought to be placed with the centre of the back edge of its right foot exactly meeting the front edge of the sound-post, which again is generally in line with the *ff* holes; but no invariable rule can be given. Bringing the bridge farther forward weakens and softens the tone, while putting it farther back over the sound-post makes the tone harder and noisier. In a properly made violin the finger-board is higher at the back than the front; and this peculiarity must be closely followed in the fitting of the bridge, the first string being rather lower or closer to the finger-board than the other three. Looking along the finger-board from the scroll to the bridge, with the strings adjusted, is a good way to test the height and fit of the bridge.

FITTING THE SOUND-POST.

The sound-post must be fitted with great exactness, the ends being sloped so as to correspond with bulge of the breast and back of the violin. A sound-post setter can be bought for a few cents, or made by sharpening one end of the rib of an old umbrella, and forming a hook at the other. The sharp end of this simple tool is stuck into the shortest side of the sound-post near the top, which is thus conveyed through the right hole to its proper place in the interior of the violin. The withdrawing of the setter fixes the post temporarily; and it can then be shifted about, adjusted, and made more rigid by using the hooked end of the setter above or below, as may be necessary. The sound-post ought not to be too tightly fixed, so as to bulge the breast of the violin, as the pressure of the strings helps to secure it more firmly as soon as they are put on and tuned to concert pitch. The sound-post ought to be made of good pine, cut with the grain, round, and about a quarter of an inch in diameter; and the grain may run either parallel with that of the belly, or exactly across it.

GLASS SOUND-POSTS.

Some years ago there was a rage among players for sound-posts of thin glass tubing; but as they give a hollow, spurious kind of tone, they have fallen into disuse. If they be preferred, they may be ground down to the size with a file, and inserted and manipulated by fastening a string to each end, and bringing the ends of these strings out of the *ff* holes, cutting them away as soon as the post is in the most satisfactory place. The exact fit of the post may be ascertained by removing the tail-piece peg, and looking into the interior in a strong light.

FITTING THE PEGS.

The pegs of a violin ought always to be made of good box-wood. Ebony is greasy, apt to slip, and liable to crack and split; while box has a good grip, and is very tough and durable. A good set of these can be had for about twenty-five cents, and that is a trifle for a life comfort. When, through time, the pegs get so far worked into their sockets that the hole for the string gets past the centre of the box in the scroll, a new hole ought to be drilled closer to the head of the peg, and the opposite way of the wood, as the strain of the string then tends to pull the peg out of its socket, endless slipping and annoyance being the result, no matter what kind of peg is used. The pegs must be pressed in while tuning, and ought never to protrude on the opposite side of the scroll, as that interferes with the working of those on that side.

ADJUSTING THE STRINGS ON THE PEGS.

It is most important, in putting on the strings, that the ends in the box of the scroll be always twisted and brought up *towards the inside*. Thus, holding the violin in its proper position, the fourth and third strings, after being fixed with a knot in the tail-piece slots and passed through the hole in the peg, are twisted twice, and the ends brought up towards the right hand, and the other two in the reverse way. The effect of this arrangement is seen as soon as the string is tightened, as it throws the coils of the string circling the peg on that part between the hole in the peg and the side of the scroll, thus securely *locking* the peg in its place, and making slipping almost an impossibility. If this be carefully attended to, very little pressure need be made on the peg to keep it in its place while tuning,—sometimes none at all. The ends of the fourth, third, and second strings, as soon as they are adjusted and tuned, ought to be cut cleanly away, and the remaining lengths put away in a tin box. So far as economy is concerned, the same might be done with the first; but, as this string is most liable to break at an awkward moment, as a matter of expediency it is better left coiled round the scroll. It is then ready in the peg-hole to draw up and re-adjust. In doing so, all the old length should be cut away, as it will have become furred, and will produce only a dull tone, and is liable to snap very soon after being re-adjusted. In putting on strings, particularly those of silk or wire, great care must be taken not to break their smoothness, or unwind the twist by making kinks or hankles in undoing the coils. The point of the second string must be kept smooth and unbroken, the peg being far into the scroll-box, and difficult of access. As soon as the string is through the hole in this peg, and protruding a little on the other side, turn the peg slightly, and continue to press the unbroken string through the hole, when it will generally appear below, and with a turn of the peg can be caught and adjusted.

KEEP THE BRIDGE PERPENDICULAR.

When putting on strings, and at all times, be careful to keep the bridge perpendicular, as the tuning of the strings tends to draw it forward. If this be not attended to, endless breaking of bridges will be the result, to say nothing of the horrible start caused by the sudden crash, and the possible fall of the sound-post as well. This is specially to be guarded against in using rough or unpolished strings. The first string ought never to be slackened, and will last quite as long at full pitch. Being thinner than the others, it is generally fixed differently at the tail-piece. After passing the end through the hole in the peg, bring it up towards the bridge, and make a loop-knot on the end. Pass this through the hole in the tail-piece; bring it out below and up over the side; slip it under the string, there passing from bridge to hole, keeping the knot behind the ridge on the tail-piece; and then tighten carefully, and tune as usual. When one end of the string is thinner than the other, it is best to turn the thin end towards the bridge. If a string plays false, —flat or sharp,—the fault may sometimes be modified or remedied by reversing it; but as a rule this defect arises from bad gauging of the relative thickness of the strings, or from a join or knot in the string itself, formed in making, and generally invisible to the eye; or from a fault of the violin, as a false string taken from one violin will sometimes play perfectly in tune on another.

CHAPTER V.

HOLDING THE VIOLIN.

THE position of the violin in these days, when almost no limit is put to shifting but the bridge itself, is of the utmost importance, the slightest awkwardness or error of detail being sufficient to cramp the execution for life. In their directions on this point, as well as that of the holding of the bow, nearly all Violin Tutors are tantalizingly vague, and therefore misleading; the cause being, I suppose, that the typographical directions have to be crammed into the smallest possible space, or are left to be elaborated and explained by a teacher, while most prominence is given to the actual music. No such drawback exists here; and I will try to make the directions so clear and minute that mistake will be all but impossible.

The violin is held in the left hand, with the chin resting on the breast of the instrument, well over the ribs, and on the *left side* of the tail-piece. The violin is then as near as possible horizontal; the rule being that the knuckles, or second joints of the fingers of the left hand, are level with the nose of the performer. The left side of the instrument is raised to an angle of twenty-five degrees, to allow of the back strings being commanded easily with the bow without moving the violin. The broad end of the violin is placed on the left collar-bone, and as deep in under the chin as possible; the reason for this being that, after moving up the left hand to command the upper notes,—technically called "shifting,"—it is necessary to grip the violin firmly with the chin before the hand can be brought back to the first position. If this were not done, the violin would come away with the hand, and the performance come to a sudden and possibly disastrous conclusion. How to bring back the hand with ease and grace I shall show in another chapter; but here I may distinctly lay down, that the left shoulder should *at no time* approach the back of the instrument. This ungainly and uncouth habit, while shifting, is only too common even among professional players, as any one may see by getting to the left side of the violins at a public concert. This is not easy in regard to the first violins, — unless by getting into the orchestra among he singers, — as they sit with their right hand to the audience, and the second violins do not generally shift so much; but enough will be seen to bear out what I have here asserted. Only one here and there brings back the hand with a swift and all but imperceptible jerk of the wrist, while the majority will be found bringing up the left shoulder in a sneaking way at the critical moment, making the movement, not only ugly, but painful to behold.

AIDS TO HOLDING THE VIOLIN.

Nature is not always kind to the violinist, giving some small collar-bones, as she gives some sweaty hands; but *no one* need get into this clumsy habit. If no amount of practice will induce the collar-bone and chin to do their work, we may assist them in two ways; but, before noticing these, I may state that constant practice does a deal, — the collar-bone through time actually appearing to become more prominent, just as the lips of a cornet-player, when "in form," always look as if he were preparing to kiss some one. If the student be a gentleman, he may make a little pad or cushion of wool, or any soft substance, to be buttoned on to his under-shirt immediately below the collar-bone, and inclining towards the shoulder. This pad should slope in the same direction as the lappel of the waistcoat, and generally take the place of the thick collar of the every-day coat, when this is cast aside for the thin one of the full-dress swallow-tail. If this be thought ungainly or objectionable, a handkerchief may be made into a loose pad, and thrust in between the waistcoat and the shirt, though I am bound to say that that is a clumsy way of getting out of the difficulty, and one particularly offensive to the eye. Lastly, if neither of these plans be adopted, a fiddle-holder may be fixed to the violin, which makes slipping almost impossible.

FIDDLE-HOLDERS, OR CHIN-RESTS.

Spohr designed a fiddle-holder, which is fixed above the tail-piece of the violin, and thus exactly in the *centre* of the instrument. That is a fault and the true secret of this holder never having become popular, as all experience goes to show that an easy command of the back strings is attained only by keeping the chin on the left side of the tail-piece. I must say, however, that this holder has one great recommendation; that is, that it is entirely free of the instrument, and has no metal screw attached, and so cannot in the slightest degree act as a mute on the tone. If this good quality could be grafted on to a fiddle-holder, which should be placed on the left side of the tail-piece, the general adoption of that new holder would be certain. Besides the Spohr fiddle-holder, there are three others, which are screwed on to the ribs of the violin close to the tail-piece. One is a clumsy thing covered with green velvet, and having a thick pad *behind* the violin as well as above. That is an objectionable feature, as the violin is already thick enough to be grasped with ease, and there is absolutely no use for the protuberance at the back. The next holder, and the latest invention of the kind, is an oval plate of ebony about two inches broad and three inches long, somewhat hollowed in the face, which is fixed with two metal screws on the left side of the tail-piece. This holder does not touch the breast of the violin, except at the very edge above the ribs, and so does not mute the violin. But it has a patched and clumsy look, and is apt through time to get pressed down on the violin. It also necessitates the violin being held rather farther out from the collar-bone than it should be held, that the point of the chin may rest in the hollow of the holder. So, on the whole, when we remember also the liability of ebony to crack and split, this holder is not likely to prove so popular as the last I shall mention.

DESIGN FOR A NEW FIDDLE-HOLDER.

I have myself designed a holder, which, however, I have never got made or tested, as I do not use a holder myself. This is a combination of tail-piece and violin-holder. My plan is to have the holder and tail-piece cut out of one piece of ebony, the holder to be at the left side of the tail-piece, and touching the violin only on the extreme outer edge of the breastplate above the ribs, and only with three tiny feet on the wood like those on the bridge of the violin, only pointed instead of spread out at the bottom. The ridge of the holder is half an inch thick behind, and flat on the top, and has a hollow slope to fit the chin inside, as indicated in the annexed full-size diagram. It is also slightly hollowed out on the underside of the slope, that it may rise free of the breastplate of the violin, and touch it only above the ribs with the feet already mentioned.

One great advantage of this plan is, that the metal screw is abolished, — and all metal should be kept from a violin; and another is that the chin completely overlaps the holder, and rests upon the breast of the violin, which thus forms a bottom to the hollow of the chin-rest, thus affording a deeper and more secure grip of the instrument, and obviating the danger of pressing the chin-rest down on the violin. Spohr, in recommending the use of his violin-holder, objects to the chin being pressed "on the sound-board or tail-piece, thereby checking the vibration of these parts, to the detriment of the sonority and volume of tone of the instrument." The most trifling mistake in this statement is that which gives vibration to the tail-piece. Passing that over as too absurd to require answering, and referring to the alleged impeding of the vibration of the breastplate of the violin, I may say, that, after experimenting and testing in every way with dozens of violins, I have come to the con-

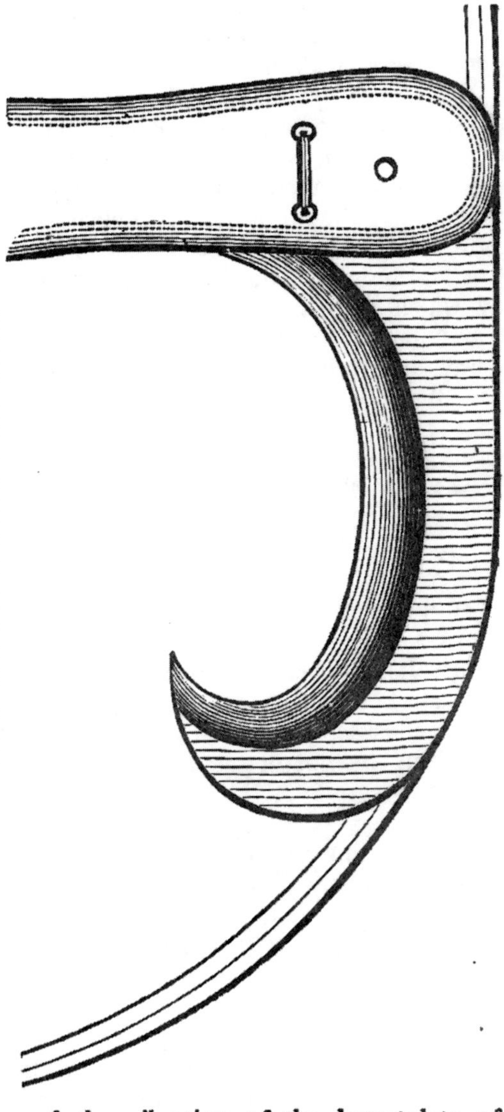

DESIGN FOR A TAIL-PIECE FIDDLE-HOLDER.

clusion that no such impeding exists, and that the chin of the performer, however firmly pressed on the breastplate, does not impede or check or enfeeble the tone, any more than does the pressure of the feet of the bridge. I have noticed also that, with a skilled player who can use the wrist in shifting down the hand, there is not so much danger of the instrument slipping forward with the hand as of it sliding imperceptibly from under the chin towards the right hand; and very good players who use no chin-rest may be seen perpetually shifting it back to its right position. This inclination of the violin to slide away in the direction of its own slope has caused me to make the end of my own design hooked, so as to catch on the left side of the chin, and prevent this incessant slipping to the right. The only objection to the design is the brittleness of ebony, which, being more beautiful and ornamental than reliable, and having the fibres running across the holder, might give way at the junction of tail-piece and chin-rest or elsewhere. A strong peg of tough wood might be run through the top of the tail-piece and the entire length of the holder, firmly glued into a hole drilled before the cutting-out of the design; or the whole might be made of papier-maché, which is brighter and less brittle than ebony; but I am not sure if this last material would stand the strain of the strings on the tail-piece.

As there may be difficulty, and probably expense, in the way of the adoption of my design, which some players may not care to face, I may notice, lastly, a fiddle-holder which, though far from perfect, is the best at present made and sold. This is one which is screwed on in the same way as the green velvet one, but which consists of a narrow ridge of ebony or papier-maché running from the nut of the tail-piece, on which it catches, to the left-hand corner of the top of the violin. This holder is flat behind, has a neat appearance, does not perceptibly mute the violin, and, though not hooked to prevent side slipping, is a great boon to many players. In conclusion, I may state that Madame Neruda uses no fiddle-holder; and would advise the student not to adopt one, until he is quite certain that he cannot master the instrument without its aid.

THE POSITION OF THE SHOULDER.

We have now adjusted the violin so far as the chin and collarbone are concerned. Let us turn our attention to the position of the left shoulder, arm, and hand. The first fault which a teacher generally notices is, that the student holds the instrument too far back against the left shoulder, which would necessitate him playing the bow over his shoulder, and make it literally impossible for him to draw a full-length bow while keeping the bow in a line parallel with the bridge during its entire passage across the strings. Nor is this fault confined to mere pupils. I have met many professionals who deliberately play with the violin against the shoulder, the result of which is that, when the point of the bow is used, it is, instead of running parallel with the bridge, describing an angle as acute as the forks of the letter V. To escape this difficulty I lately noticed one holding the bow some inches from the bottom of the hair, thus shortening it and depriving it of so much of its power, and creating a new defect, instead of applying the real remedy. To overcome this tendency is a somewhat painful process; but, as it must be done, it ought to be boldly attacked from the first. The left arm is brought forward till the elbow is directly below the body of the instrument, the left shoulder being moved slightly forward to accommodate the arm in its new position. As this contortion is a little painful at first, when long continued, a second fault will probably spring from it. The student will try to relieve the fatigue of the arm and shoulder by allowing the elbow to rest on his own ribs. This is not allowed, and, indeed, cannot be done if the rule to keep the knuckles of the left hand level with nose of the performer be sedulously attended to. There is a reason for every thing in violin-playing, and that for this is that the violin when held nearly horizontal supports the bow without any action of the fingers of the right hand; while, if the elbow be allowed to rest on the front of the student's ribs, there is formed a slope on the string, and the weight of the bow naturally makes it slip away from the bridge towards the fingers and scroll. The fingers and wrist of the right hand have enough work of their own to perform, as the student will discover, without saddling them with the task of keeping the bow in its place on the string.

THE POSITION OF THE HAND AND WRIST.

The elbow of the left arm being brought well forward under the instrument, and kept from touching the body, the student may turn his attention to his hand and wrist. Most Violin Tutors simply tell him to hold the neck of the violin "between the third joint of the first finger and the thumb,"—a direction so vague as to become positively misleading. The violin is *not* held at the third joint of the first finger, and "the thumb" is too indefinite, and might mean any place between the point and the socket. If the student will look at the inside of the first finger of his left hand, and count the third crease from the point, he will get the exact place at which to place the corner edge of the finger-board of the violin, close to the little bit of ebony called the nut, over which the strings pass into the box of the scroll. This crease is not a joint. The third joint, indeed, is half an inch farther down, and is marked by a crease which runs right across the whole hand. The opposite side of the neck of the violin rests *on*, not against, the fleshy part of the thumb, between its point and the crease marking the first joint. The result of this arrangement is, that sufficient space is left in the fork of the thumb below the neck, through which the point of the bow might be freely passed. By resting the neck *on* the thumb instead of against it, the whole of the fingers are brought over the strings, which may be commanded far up on the fourth string without the slightest contorting or inconvenience.

Unless this position is acquired, a good shake, whether close or open, is an impossibility; and shifting, instead of being a pleasing change, becomes a dreaded task. To facilitate this freedom in commanding the strings,—especially with regard to the fourth finger, the shortest of all,—the wrist of the left hand is turned well out, so as not to touch the neck or ribs of the violin. The wrist, indeed, ought not to touch the violin at all until the third position is reached.

The hand and wrist are now in their proper position, the neck of the violin resting on the fleshy part of the thumb, with that member kept well below it to support the weight of that end of the violin, and leave the rest of the hand comparatively free of contact, the point of the thumb on no account to rise above the back edge of the finger-board. The wrist being kept straight, and the whole of the hand being so sunk that the space already alluded to at the fork of the thumb and forefinger is clearly defined, the gratifying result will at once appear. The whole of the fingers are brought nearer the strings, and the little finger, or fourth, as it is called, and which every beginner pathetically bewails as too short, is found to be quite long enough to reach B, E, A, or D, without the slightest wriggling or moving of hand or wrist. As the pupil progresses, indeed, and the hand becomes set to the position, he will find that practice will enable him to stretch easily, in certain passages, a semitone or a whole tone above these notes with the same much-despised little finger, no matter how short and stumpy it may appear, which, with the violin held in the third joint of the first finger, is an impossibility. I once detected this fault in a very diligent student, who had spent many a hard-earned guinea on a teacher who knew perfectly well the principle which I am here trying to demonstrate, and who therefore must have wilfully kept his pupil in ignorance. I was not teaching him, but playing with him and some other amateurs, and chanced to notice a peculiar jerking and wriggling of his hand every time he used his fourth finger. I examined his hand, and found the neck of the instrument sunk into the fork of the thumb, literally below the third joint of the finger; and how difficult it is to get the little finger to even approach the finger-board with the hand in that position, any player or student may easily ascertain for himself by testing. I tried to correct the curious blunder, but was innocently met with the rejoinder, "It should be held between the third joint of the first finger and the thumb, shouldn't it?" and it took me some time, with practical illustrations of the evils of the habit, to set him right. That student is now a teacher; and I hope he is grateful to me for the hint, which cost neither of us any thing, but at once laid the foundation of a rapid advancement on his part, which otherwise would have been impossible.

I have now put the holding of the violin as clearly as I can before the student, and would merely say in conclusion, that, to acquire freedom and ease,—complete mastery, in fact, of the instrument,—he must (1) keep the socket or fork of the thumb well sunk from the neck, (2) the weight of the violin resting chiefly *on* the thumb, (3) the hand well over the finger-board, (4) the knuckles of the fingers turned out squarely, that the points of the fingers may fall perpendicularly on the strings, and (5) the wrist from touching the ribs or neck of the violin.

SETTING THE HAND TO THE POSITION.

To set the hand to this position, nothing is better than practising a great deal upon the fourth string, first with all four fingers on the first position, and then, as the student advances to the shifts, as far up the string as he can reach. That is the only—and, I may add, an infallible—method of setting the hand and gaining great power and freedom. In the second part of Henning's "First Book for the Violin," there are several excellent exercises suitable for this purpose; and in the fourth part of Campagnoli's "Method for the Violin," page 105, there is an exercise for the fourth string which every advanced student ought to have beside him, and practise occasionally till his left hand feels ready to drop in pieces. The second and fifth variations in De Beriot's "Second Air Varied" may be used for the same purpose.

THE ATTITUDE OF THE PLAYER.

There is rather more freedom in playing standing than sitting; but both ways always ought to be diligently practised. Sitting or standing, the head must be kept erect, and the chest well expanded. When standing, it is best to rest the weight of the body chiefly on the left foot. Avoid swaying the body, or moving uneasily from one foot to the other,—a fidgety habit only too easily contracted. The music-stand ought to be opposite the right breast, and the violin and left hand consequently pointing over its left side; but in solo playing the performer, if he *must* use a music-stand, ought to place it sufficiently to the left side to allow an uninterrupted view of himself by every one in the room. When sitting, the player must not cross his legs or lean forward, but place both feet on the floor, pressing the chair back with his shoulder-blades only.

CHAPTER VI.

THE MANAGEMENT OF THE BOW.

THE mastery of the bow is the perfection of grace and delicate art. Without it no student, however hard working, need hope for that endless variety of expression and subtle swelling and diminishing of tone which places the violin above every musical instrument. With it success is almost sure.

BALANCING THE BOW.

The bow is held balanced between the thumb and the first and fourth fingers of the right hand. Any student may analyze the position and management for himself by placing the inner side of the point of his thumb, about the middle of the nail, on the stick close to the little silver ferule binding the hair in the nut, sloping towards the heel of the bow in exactly the line of the fourth finger, the point of the little finger on the *top* of the stick, about an inch and a half behind the thumb, and the first joint of the first finger on the *front* of the stick, about an inch before the thumb. He will now have the bow perfectly balanced without the aid of the two middle fingers at all.

Let him now bring down the two middle fingers easily between the first and fourth, slightly apart, and sloping gracefully towards the heel of the bow so as to show no angular joints or knuckles; turn out the first joint of the thumb till the back of that member, close to the outer corner of the root of the nail, presses against the edge of the hair close to the nut, and the position is perfect. He will now find that the thumb is exactly opposite the second finger; that the stick of the bow runs across the first joint and towards the second joint of the first finger in a slanting direction; across the fleshy part of the points of the second and third fingers in front of the first joint,

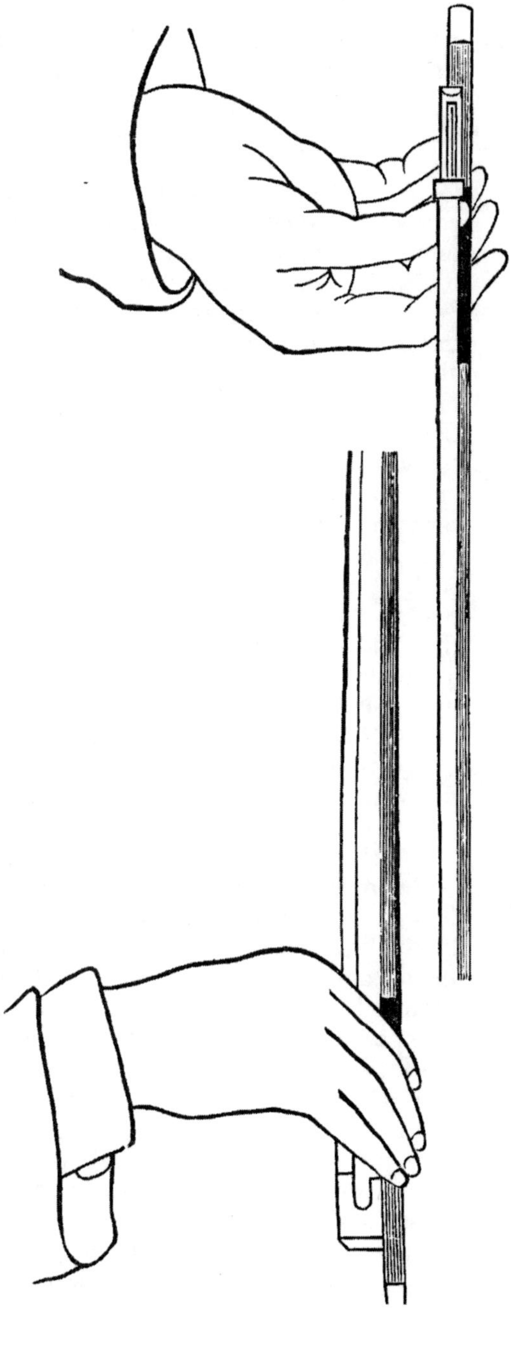

to the point of the little finger, which, being shorter, lies naturally, and as an important balancing lever, on the top of the stick, instead of hanging over the front like the other three.

The diagrams opposite will give some idea of the position of the fingers on the bow as seen from the front and the back. In Spohr's "Violin School" somewhat similar diagrams will be found; but they are in some of the minute details not strictly correct. I would suggest that in some future edition new or improved drawings of the hand should be subsituted for those of Spohr which have been retained. Figure I., plate 3, in Spohr's work, is incorrect, inasmuch as the stick of the bow, instead of inclining from the performer, lies perpendicular above the string; Fig. III. is an exceedingly clumsy representation, but gives a good idea of the position of the thumb on the stick; and Fig. IV., though giving an excellent idea of the turning out of the joint of the thumb against the hair, is altogether wrong in having the third finger longer instead of shorter than the second, and also in having the little finger drooping over the stick instead of having its point on the top of the stick as represented (plate 2) in Holiday's graceful full-length figure, which in turn is out of drawing in having the bow shorter than the violin. I am careful to point out these things, not, as some clever critic may imagine, with any idea of placing myself before the greatest teacher of the violin who ever lived, but simply that the student may not be led by the incorrect drawings to form habits which Spohr himself most vigorously denounces.

THE WORK OF THE FIRST AND FOURTH FINGERS.

Before analyzing further the management of the bow, it may be well to impress upon the student the important parts played by the first and fourth fingers. The bow is held between the thumb and the second finger, aided by the first and third, and balanced by the fourth. The first finger lies easily on the stick, a little in advance of the principal holding members, and has for its work chiefly the graduation of the pressure of the bow on the string. If a note or a passage be wished soft, the first finger merely assists the others in a subordinate manner to draw the bow smoothly and lightly across the string; but, when a swell or a loud note is required, the pressure of the first finger is increased, the result of which is that the hair of the bow, which, owing to the turning-out of the first joint of the thumb, has been touching the string only with its outer edge, is now forced flat on the string like a broad white tape, and so grips more of the string, and causes a stronger vibration and louder tone. The first finger, indeed, is sole master of all the pressure applied to the strings, and for this reason must lie so easily on the stick, that, when a long down bow is drawn, the stick moves from the first joint of this finger nearly into the second. The fourth, or little finger, in turn plays the important part of bearing on its point the whole weight of the stick, and is thus an important ally of the first finger when a soft tone is required, as by pressing it strongly on the stick—the thumb being the fulcrum, or centre of leverage—the bow may be all but lifted from the string. The beginner, then, must be particularly careful (1) that the thumb is kept opposite the second finger, and close to the ferule of the nut; (2) that the first finger lies easily on the stick, and, in taking long bows, allow the stick to slip from the first to the second joint of the finger, and *vice versa;* (3) that the point of the little finger lies on the top of the stick, leaving it only when the extreme point of the bow is used; (4) that the fingers lie slightly apart on the stick, sloped gracefully towards the heel of the bow; and (5) that the first joint of the thumb be turned out till the edge of the hair touches the back of the thumb, close to the outer corner of the root of the nail.

THE POSITION OF THE HAIR ON THE STRINGS.

The bow may now be placed on an open string, when it will be found, if these directions have been strictly followed, that the stick of the bow is inclining towards the finger-board and neck of the violin, with only the outer edge of the hair touching the string, instead of its whole width lying flat on the string, as a novice would naturally think correct. This is the proper position of the bow, and must never be altered. If the whole width of the hair be required, a slight pressure of the first finger of the right hand on the stick will instantly bring about that result, without the stick itself being brought perpendicular above the string. There is in this seemingly unaccountable and curious freak the great secret of good violin-playing. It is difficult to make this clear to a beginner by mere words: but the fact will gradually be revealed to him as he advances, (1) that the spring in the bow is not only stronger, but more easily managed, when the stick is inclined from the bridge; (2) that a soft tone is most easily produced by using only the edge of the hair, and at the same time playing a little further from the bridge; and (3) that a swell, or *crescendo* and *diminuendo*, on one note can be produced only by using the edge of the hair when beginning the note, gradually increasing the pressure of the first finger on the stick as it approaches the centre till the whole of the hair lies flat on the string, and then gradually diminishing the pressure till at the other end of the bow the edge only of the hair is again in action. It is the rule with all stringed instruments to incline the stick of the bow from the bridge; thus we find that with the violoncello and double bass, which are played upside down, the stick is inclined towards the players instead of from them, as in the violin. That there is a good and scientific reason for this I have not a doubt; but I have not yet heard one advanced that quite satisfied me. I once had a pupil who played the violoncello before he came to me to study the violin; and, though I drilled him steadily, I failed to altogether break him of the habit of inclining the stick towards him.

USING THE BOW.

Having got an intelligent idea of the position of the fingers on the bow into his head, the student may now try to draw the bow its full length across the string. The result ought to be a long, smooth, full-toned note; but the probability is that it will be so rough and scratchy, that even the eager student himself will stop and say, "Well, isn't that horrible?" In the first place, it is probable that he will be pressing the bow on the string with the weight of the whole hand, and pushing it *into* the string instead of drawing it steadily over it. If the hair be properly rosined, very little pressure is required to make the violin vibrate; and, as power of tone is not of the greatest importance to a beginner, he may content himself at first with a smooth note rather than a loud one.

The following advice, given more than a hundred years ago by the celebrated Tartini to a lady pupil, should be written in letters of gold: "Your first study should be the true manner of holding, balancing, and pressing the bow lighfly, but steadily, upon the string, in such a manner that *it shall seem to breathe* the first tone it gives, which must proceed from the friction of the bow, and not from percussion, as by a blow given with a hammer upon it. This depends upon laying the bow lightly upon the strings at the first contact, and on gently pressing it afterwards, which, if done gradually, can scarcely have too much force given to it, because, if the tone is begun with delicacy, there is little danger of rendering it afterwards coarse or harsh. Of this first contact and delicate manner of beginning a tone you should make yourself a perfect mistress in every part of the bow, — as well in the middle as at the extremities, and in moving it up as well as down."

The above advice is too often disregarded even by professional players, some of whom we may see perpetually laying the bow on the string, letting it rest there and "bite" the string, and then rendering out the note like saw-sharpeners. The sound thus produced is noise, not music.

But a still greater fault than that of a scratchy note will probably be discovered. The hair ought to move across the string about an inch from the bridge *during its entire passage.* In doing so it ought to describe a line as straight as the bridge itself, not forming the slightest curve. This objectionable curve will be the first thing that the student will detect in his bowing. Why there should be no curve is easily explained. When the bow moves straight across the string, it sets the fibres of the string into even vibration, and through that the fibres of the breast of the violin, which run straight in the same direction; when a curve is formed in crossing, the vibrations become ragged and interrupted, as if the bow were tending to split the string at an angle instead of straight up the middle, and the immediate consequence is that the tone is impaired. Straight bowing is the great indispensable of good playing. Hundreds of players never acquire it; and dozens even of professional players fondly imagine they have it when they have it not. Again, some students acquire it, like the staccato bow, almost without an effort; while others can only master the difficulty by long and patient investigation, watchfulness, and hard work. I am thus drawing the student's attention to the defect from the first, that the evil habit may never be formed; which brings us to consider the action of the wrist of the right hand.

THE ACTION OF THE WRIST.

If the student, in drawing the bow from heel to point across the string, will keep his eye on the wrist of his right hand, or will watch any good player doing so, he will find that, to keep the hair and stick in a line parallel with the bridge, it is necessary when the heel of the bow is on the string to have the outside of the wrist bent upwards, which bend must be gradually decreased and altered as the bow descends till, when the point of the bow lies on the string, the position is completely reversed;

the inside of the wrist now being bent outwards towards the ground, and the hand inclining upwards. This action of the wrist takes place with every stroke of the bow, however short. In quick passages, in which the shortest possible stroke of the bow is required for each note, the motion proceeds entirely from the wrist, the whole arm being kept perfectly still, except in so far as it is necessary to use it to raise or depress the bow in passing from one string to another. A free and flexible wrist is therefore a great boon to the student. Practice with the bow soon produces the desirable freedom; and the flexibility may be increased by occasionally flapping the hand rapidly back and forward,—that is, shaking it on the joint without the bow, first up and down, and then from side to side.

In longer bows—technically called "half-strokes"—the motion must proceed entirely from the wrist and the lower part of the arm; the upper part, from elbow to shoulder, being kept as still as possible, and as close to the side as it can be kept with convenience in playing on the back strings. Some teachers have the insane idea that the upper part of the arm should never leave the side, and make their pupils practise with a book held between that and the side; but how absurd is this craze may be proved by any one who chooses to watch any of our great soloists—as Joachim, Neruda, Vieutemps, Sainton, or Carrodus—when playing on the back strings. They do not—and could not, consistently with grace and freedom—hold the upper part of the arm *always* close to the side; and where these masters, who have made the instrument the sole study of their lives, do not lead, the student may safely hesitate to follow. Holding the arm rigidly against the side induces a kind of "cat's-paw" style of holding the bow and bending of the wrist, and, far from being more graceful, makes the performer look as if he suffered from some deformity or malformation of the wrist and body.

TO ACQUIRE A GRACEFUL STYLE.

To acquire a perfect and graceful style of bowing, I know no plan better than that I am about to suggest. I once said to the great comedian, Mr. J. L. Toole, "How is it that you manage to set people a-laughing before you open your mouth? Where do you get such comical looks and turns and expression of face, eyes, and mouth?" His answer was characteristic, and may teach many an aspiring student who fancies that greatness is reached without hard work. "I get them in the looking-glass," said Mr. Toole. "I sometimes sit for two hours at a time doing nothing but making faces before a mirror." From this admission the student of the violin may take a valuable hint: he must spend hours practising his bowing before a looking-glass. Let him place the glass or mirror at his right side,— not in front of him,—and the bow on an open string; then let him allow his chin for the moment to leave its place on the breast of the instrument, that he may turn his head to look into the glass at the reflected bow. He will there see a faithful and unflattering picture of his bow during its entire passage across the string; and, if he does not learn enough to take the conceit out of him, he must either be a wonderfully apt pupil, or not applying the test rightly. It is a crucial test, which I invite all, whether amateur or professional, to apply to themselves.

USING THE FULL LENGTH OF THE BOW.

In addition to practising beside a mirror, I would impress on the beginner the necessity of drawing the bow to its full length, and not merely twiddling away with about a third of its length like some street-players. Don't be afraid to throw out your arm if you would produce a good tone. The bow, when drawn slowly or hesitatingly, seems to act as a kind of damper on the string: at least, a swiftly flashed bow produces a smoother, mellower, and more brilliant tone. Of course I do not mean the student to understand that long bows suit all kinds of music; but the ability to draw the full length of the bow is not easily acquired, and ought to be sedulously cultivated from the first. In practising the long stroke, both up and down, no particular music need be used. Any of the open strings may be persistently sawed upon, as in the early exercises in Spohr, the mirror being at his right side, and his eye fixed upon the reflection of the bow and his wrist in the glass. He will then find that the position at which the bow is most apt to begin to describe a curve is when the point of the bow is nearing the string, and the hand of the student therefore farthest from his side, to obviate which he must allow the point of the little finger, simultaneously with the slipping of the stick from the first joint of the first finger into the second joint, to leave the stick for the moment, allowing it gradually to resume its place as the bow moves back in the opposite direction, and the stick regains its place in the first joint of the first finger. He will also find that there is a tendency in the stick, when the point approaches the strings, to alter its angle from inclining towards the finger-board to a more perpendicular position. These, and numberless other faults, the unflattering mirror will enable him to correct better than if he had a dozen teachers to report to him how he is doing. The test is within the reach of all, and the truthfulness of the report can never be doubted.

CHAPTER VII.

TUNING THE VIOLIN.

THE violin is tuned by fifths. It is usual to tune the second string to an A pitch-pipe or tuning-fork; then to tune the third string five notes lower, that is, to D; then the fourth string five notes lower than D; and then the first string a fifth above A: thus,—

The beginner has sometimes a little difficulty in tuning his instrument perfectly; but the ear very soon becomes accustomed to the sound of a perfect fifth. If serious difficulty be experienced at first, a temporary line may be drawn with a lead pencil across the finger-board of the violin at that place where the fourth finger falls, which may be found by running up five notes on one of the strings. Then, after tuning the second string to A, place the little finger firmly upon it at the mark, and the sound given forth should be in perfect unison with the first string, if that string be in tune. Then place the fourth finger on the third string at the mark; and, when the third string is in tune, it will give a sound in unison with the second; follow the same plan with the fourth, and something like a perfect tuning will be the result. To train the ear the student must now draw the bow to its full length, up and down, on two strings,—first on the second and third; then on the second and first; and then on the third and fourth. The practising of the straight bow beside the mirror, and the training of the ear to the sound of the fifth, may proceed together; care being taken that the violin, being for the moment deprived of the support of the chin, through the student turning his head to look into the mirror, does not alter its position on the collar-bone.

The diagram of the finger-board of the violin, given at the beginning of the book, may now be studied carefully as far up as the notes D (fourth string, fourth finger), A (third string, fourth finger), E (second string, fourth finger), and B (first string, fourth finger), which is as far up as the fingers in the natural or first position can command. Those higher up, which I have drawn in a somewhat smaller character, may be studied, and will be referred to more particularly in the chapter treating of shifting. The letters indicate the exact spot on the finger-board on which the points of the fingers must be placed to stop the string, and produce the notes of the natural scale on every position and on every string. The smaller white spots, without name, show where the semitones, flat or sharp, are to be found. In a strictly scientific sense, there is a difference between a flat and a sharp on the violin; and to produce that difference it is the rule to play a sharp with the finger advanced or pushed nearer the bridge, and a flat with the finger drawn back nearer the nut: but the difference is so inappreciable to the eye, that for all practical purposes the same spot may suffice, and be less confusing to the student.

The diagram might be cut out and pasted on the finger-board of the violin as a guide to the student's fingers; but as I have taken it from a full-sized Stradiuarius, and one which is considered wide in the fingering, it is possible that it would not exactly suit his violin. Violins vary greatly in the length of string required between the bridge and the net; and the "stepping" is proportionately wider or closer, as much as a quarter of an inch of difference sometimes being found in two instruments in the fingering of the first fifth.

Besides, it is a bad habit to look much at the fingers, and it is better that the student should get a clear and intelligent idea of the position of the notes on the finger-board into his *head* than have it pasted on his violin; and it is chiefly for that purpose that the diagram is given. It will be observed that the spots or spaces, on which the finger-points are placed to produce the notes, get gradually closer as they ascend the finger-board: so that, while a whole tone requires the fingers to be fully an inch apart at the nut, it requires only half that distance from F to G on the shift, and little more than a quarter from F to G in alt. This fact, necessitating the finger-points being gradually brought closer as we ascend the shift, need not stagger the pupil, as by the time he comes to play on the shift his ear will have become so trained to musical sounds, that his fingers will fall almost instinctively into their proper position. On some of the very high positions it is necessary, in playing semitones, to lift one finger before the other can be got down into its proper place; and, when a thorough mastery of the instrument is attained, it is usual, in playing a chromatic run — generally with a staccato bow — to simply put one finger — generally the fourth — firmly down on the high note, and draw it by small degrees backwards on the strings till it lands on D on the third position, or B on the first position, when the remainder of the run may be fingered in the ordinary manner.

THE PRACTICE OF SCALES.—THE LONG BOW.

Having learned to tune his instrument, and draw a straight long bow, the pupil may now begin the practice of scales. The long straight bow must be here continued, and on no account should the student attempt to play the notes fast. He must also be sure to turn the first joints of the fingers of the left hand squarely out, so that the point and not the front of the finger shall press on the string. If the flat of the finger were used, a painful corn would be the result; while, when the point is used, all the hard skin which is formed drops off of its own accord without pain or inconvenience, and a much better tone is produced. The finger-points must be pressed firmly on the string, that no part of the string, but that between the finger and the bridge, may have the slightest chance to vibrate. It is best to begin with the scale of G, and to practise it steadily with long, smooth bows, from G to B and back again, till something like firmness of fingering and purity of intonation is obtained. Rather more difficulty is generally experienced by the beginner in coming down the scale than in going up; and, if any fault more than another is likely to appear, it will be carelessness or slovenliness in the stopping of the semitones. These ought to be sharply defined, as this habit is apt to cling to the pupil for life, particularly when he comes to play a semitone close to the nut, which will almost certainly be played a little sharp. For the semitones the fingers must be kept perfectly close, — as close as they can be placed without lifting. Let particular attention be paid to them; take care of the semitones, and the whole tones will take care of themselves; and when any note is stopped falsely, or out of tune, pause at once, and move the finger up or down till it is righted.

THE HALF-STROKE.

When the long bow has been well practised, the half-stroke may be tried, still using the simple scale as the means. In using the long bow the upper part of the arm is slightly used as well as the lower part, wrist, and hand; in half-strokes only the lower part and wrist are used, the upper part being kept still, except in raising or depressing the bow to command the different strings. The half-stroke is used for all kinds of crisp, sharp notes; a very good specimen being the common polka. If the student will measure off the length of the hair of his bow into four quarters, and then use the two middle quarters of that to produce the note, playing it with a brisk jerk of the arm, he will have a good idea of the half-stroke. The half-stroke may be used at any part of the bow; but, as the tone is most equal at the centre, the student may begin with the two middle quarters. In playing the scale with the half-stroke he may give each note of the scale two strokes of the bow.

THE SHORT STROKE.

Now comes the crowning difficulty, the short stroke. For this the wrist alone is employed, both parts of the arm being kept still, except for depressing or raising the bow. To acquire the necessary freedom of the wrist the student may place the upper third part of the bow on an open string, or a stopped note, and saw away at it as rapidly as his wrist will move, after the style in which "ghost music" is played in the theatre. Then he may turn to his scale again, and, giving each note four quick wrist-strokes of the bow, practise it persistently up and down; then give each note eight strokes rather quicker, till something like a flexible wrist is begun to be developed.

THE USE OF THE FOURTH FINGER.

In practising the scale at first it is usual to omit the use of the fourth finger of the left hand, except on the first string, as the open string above it produces the same note; but as it is *absolutely necessary* to use this finger in all proper playing, and it is the weakest of the fingers, its use cannot be too early begun by the student. In coming *down* the scale it ought always to be used; and, as a beginner is sometimes at a loss to know where the fourth finger should be used, I may say that a good and almost invariable rule is to use it when the note before and the note after are both *below* the open string note. Thus, if the student had to play D on the second string, and then E, and then D again, he would play the E with the fourth finger to avoid a harsh and ugly crossing on to the open first string, and as harsh a return to the second for the D. In playing rapid downward runs, slurred in one bow, and in playing chromatic, or semitone runs, either up or down, the fourth finger is almost always used. Most beginners imagine that their little finger is too short; but, if the hand be well sunk from the neck of the violin, as described in Chapter V., he will find it quite long enough not only to command the duplicate of the open string note, but, with practice, to stretch in an emergency a semitone or a whole tone higher.

A SURE MODE OF MASTERING THE BOW.

At this stage I would impress upon the student the necessity of practising persistently with the *upper half* of his bow. All rapid music, which is bowed and not slurred, ought to be played with this part; all that is fine and delicate in violin-playing is found in the upper half of the bow. The pearly staccato bow drops inert, lumpy, and all but powerless the moment it passes that Rubicon; and one great master has truly said, that, if the upper half of the bow be but practised daily and hourly for a year or two, certain mastery of the instrument will be the result. Spohr also recognizes this important fact, and gives whole exercises in short, rapid notes for the upper part of the bow alone. The lower part, indeed, is quite able to take care of itself. The whole weight of the bow there rests upon the string, as well as the weight of the hand: the tone is therefore harsh, strong, and lumpy; and for that reason the lower part is used only when the short stroke is wanted crisp, loud, and noisy. It is so much more within the command of the beginner, however, that the chances are great that he not only learns to play quick music with that part, but is quite unable to break off the habit when years and experience show him his error. To any one who may have formed the evil habit of playing too much with the heel of the bow I would say that he may be gradually weaned from the error by playing first nearer the middle of the bow, then in the middle, and then with the upper third part.

It must be distinctly understood that I am now speaking only of rapid music which is bowed and not slurred. Any one may test the difference in the tone by playing a quick passage or tune — say, a Scotch reel or a hornpipe — first with the heel of the bow, and then with the upper half. The first rendering will be harsh, grating, and unwieldy; the second, fine, smooth-flowing, clear, springy, and neat, — every note, no matter how rapid the tune, ringing out clear as a bell.

THE TIME TO PRACTISE.

The time that the student should practise daily can be decided only by himself; but it is better to practise three separate half-hours or hours than for the same time at once. The joints of the body being relaxed and looser in the morning, that is the best time to break the labor of the day, and set the hand by an hour's practice. When I was young I used to rise at six o'clock, and play steadily for two hours before breakfast; and I can recommend the practice as both healthful and beneficial.

THE PRACTISING OF EASY MELODIES AND DUETS.

Although exercises for the first few years should form the staple practice of the student, he must have from the first a few books of simple melodies to brighten and enliven the study. Constant playing at exercises induces a stiff mechanical style. White's book of one hundred "Ballads," or "English and Irish Melodies," or "Irish and Scotch Melodies," or "Operatic Melodies," each fifty cents, are excellent for this purpose at the earliest stages of the study. They are well arranged; and, where any simple shifting is required, the fingering is carefully marked. White's "Airs with Variations" (price fifty cents) is another capital book, combining melody with practice. Lastly, I may mention a cheap collection of operatic and other airs, published by Jean White, Boston, Mass., under the title of the "Violinist." These will give the student a good idea of the effect of a simple selection. The arrangements are effective, and the numbers progressive in difficulty.

CHAPTER VIII.

THE BEST KEYS TO BEGIN WITH.

THE order of progression in the different keys which I have always found most beneficial to the student is to begin with the key of G, or one sharp; then take D, two sharps, and A, three sharps; stop there, and go back to C, the natural key; and, when the first finger is accustomed to the position close to the nut necessary for playing the natural F on the first string, give the student F, or one flat, having the same fingering on the second string, and B flat, having the same fingering on the third string. The key of E, four sharps, E flat, three flats, and A flat, four flats, may then follow by degrees. I am well aware that *in theory* it is best to begin with the natural key, as I said in Chapter II.; but theory and practice are very different things, as any one will discover who tries to teach a difficult instrument like the violin. This order of the keys I would strongly recommend to the student, no matter from what violin school he may be studying. The three first-mentioned keys are so easy that the most despairing or slow pupil is cheered and animated by the progress he is making. When the first scale is mastered, and one or two simple preludes and exercises, and some easy tune is given him, such as "Home, Sweet Home," or the "Blue Bells of Scotland," he actually realizes the fact that he can play, and draws a long breath of satisfaction and delight, like the schoolboy who has mastered the first declension of Latin nouns, and can decline *mensa* perfectly, and, knowing nothing of the other declensions to follow, thinks the worst is over. Then there is no tendency to *shiftiness* in the position of the left hand, and consequent false intonation, and some attention can be paid to the movements and management of the bow. The difficulties of the journey to perfection are thus from the beginning veiled with flowers, and an enthusiasm gradually kindled sufficient to carry the student through the severest studies, and over the most trying obstacles.

PLAYING STRETCHED NOTES.

As the student's hand should now be well set to the instrument, he should have little difficulty in stretching for the high C without moving the hand. As there is always a tendency to play any notes stretched from the first position a slight degree flat, or to impart to them a whining, squeaky sound, different from that of their companions, it is best for the student to practise stretching more than a semitone. The following progessive exercises may be taken by degrees, four notes being played to each bow, and the phrase being repeated as long as the fingers will move, never passing to another until the first is mastered. In the whole four the first finger is to be kept firmly on the string, and never moved, even when the fourth has to stretch to C sharp. If the fourth finger absolutely refuses to stretch the required distance, *pull it up* with the right hand, and keep it on the string for a few moments without playing, and by degrees it will get inured to the task.

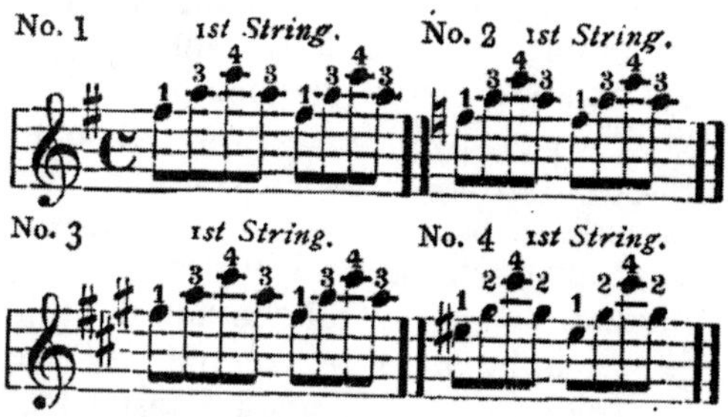

The first exercise here given will be found comparatively easy; the second, difficult; the third, comparatively easy; and the fourth, very difficult: but the immediate result will be the easy and correct stretching for the Cs. If the student will only remember to play this page, and all such passages, with the upper half of the bow, or even in some cases with the upper third part, I can assure him of success in the mastery of all that is fine and delicate in violin-playing, so far at least as the bow is concerned; but if once the fatal habit, so easily contracted, of using the under part, or heel, is acquired, it will prove a clog upon his playing for life.

POSITION OF THE RIGHT ELBOW.

Care must be taken in crossing to the back strings not to raise the elbow of the right arm too high. When playing on the first string, the cuff of the right sleeve should, during the entire passage of the bow, be as close to the side of the performer as it can move without touching or catching. When the notes are marked *staccato*, as in some of these exercises, the bow must be raised from the string between each note, so as to bounce or dance on the string,—a difficult feat with the upper half of the bow, especially in a succession of quick, short strokes, for which the wrist alone of the right hand is moved. Practice will soon overcome the difficulty, however, without having recourse to the fatally facile under half of the bow.

FIRM FINGERING.

The student, no matter how rapid the passage, must remember to finger the notes firmly by pressing the points of the fingers well down on the string as indicated in the last chapter. The nails of the left hand, for this reason, should always be short of the flesh, and neatly rounded with a nail-trimmer, so that no sharp edges or corners may be left to cut the strings.

THE ART OF SHIFTING.

As early as possible in his studies the pupil should boldly strike out and attack the shifting, by which not only may two octaves be added to the compass of the instrument, but a much greater equality of tone and variety of expression be got even on the back strings; the last consideration being immensely more important than the first. The easiest shift to play upon, the most extensive used of any in the finger-board, and the surest of attack, is beyond all question the third position; namely, that in which the first finger on the first string is advanced towards the bridge till it falls upon A instead of F. The moment this position is gained, the wrist touches the ribs or outer edge of the instrument for the first time, which is a capital guide to the hand. Moreover, this position is practically a double one; for, by extending the little finger and allowing it to lie lightly on the string, without pressing it close on the finger-board, the harmonic E in the middle of the string is produced, thus making the position almost equal to the third and fourth combined. For these reasons I think the third position should be the first attacked. Theory starts in horror, and says, "What of the second position? You should surely give that before the third?" But Theory is a bullying tyrant, who needs a little healthy snubbing occasionally. The second position is as easy to play upon as any *when you are on it;* but it is the most difficult of attack on the finger-board: therefore we may calmly put it and theory aside for the time, and go on with what will most benefit the student. When the third position is mastered on all the strings, including the harmonics got by stretching, the fifth position may follow; that is, that in which the first finger on the first string is advanced to stop C instead of A. The student will observe that the shifts are each two notes higher than the former position, and may from the first as well understand that this mode of progession is found easiest in all shifting, however intricate or rapid. There are exceptions; but that is the rule. Thus, in making an ordinary run from the first position, no matter on what string, it is usual to advance by the third, fifth, seventh, and ninth positions, and so on successively. When it is necessary to run on the other positions, it is best to get on to one of the even numbers, say the second position, and then progress upwards in the same order; that is, second, fourth, sixth, eighth, and other positions successively. For this reason I have, in the diagram of the positions given at the beginning of the book, marked them in two classes at different sides of the finger-board. Those with the odd numbers are certainly those most used by the very greatest of players; but it is necessary to practise both diligently, as a passage, or open shake, or arpeggio may occur in music at any moment, which is absolutely impossible of execution on the shifts with the odd numbers, but which may be performed with the utmost ease upon the other. On the seventh position, I may remark, the student, as on the third, really commands two positions, as, by stretching the fourth finger and letting it lie on the string without pressing it close to the finger-board, he commands the harmonic B, E, A, or D, according to the string upon which he is playing. It is common also, when on the fifth position, to stretch for the high G, or even A, when it can be done distinctly and without whining. Stretching or departing from the strict rules of fingering is indeed very easy and common on the upper positions, on account of the fingers lying much closer together. It is at this stage that the student will practically realize the advantage of not having the bridge too high, as the labor for the fingers is much lighter, the "stepping" truer, and the tone more equal and pleasing.

When the student has mastered to a certain extent the third, fifth, and seventh positions, he may come back on the finger-board, and try those with the even numbers, beginning with the second. This, as I have said, is the most difficult of attack of any, as the hand has neither the ribs of the violin nor the nut at the bottom of the finger-board and the beginning of the scroll as guides, and the space between it and the first position is so trifling that the hand is apt to advance too far in making the change. Even in this critical movement, however, there is a tolerably safe and certain mode of attack as well as a risky one; and that is to advance one finger — whichever seems safest in the passage being performed — one note on the string before moving the hand at all. Then, while that note is being played, and while the finger is kept firmly on the string, bring up the whole hand to the second position. It is well, however, to accustom the eye to read and the fingers to command the notes on this position; and for that purpose I know of no more masterly or beneficial studies than Spohr's 37th, 38th, and 39th exercises. Those in St. Jacome's work, noticed below, are also excellent. Spohr's three studies, on the other hand, can be played on no other position but the second; and, as it is only such passages that a player would put into this position, these three exercises are doubly valuable. After the second position is tolerably well mastered, the fourth, sixth, and others with the even numbers, will present little difficulty. To take any easy piece and play it entirely upon one of the shifts, — second, third, fourth, or fifth, — never moving the hand from that position, except where the low notes on the fourth string may be required, is another excellent method of mastering and attaining familiarity with the different shifts.

One more shift there is which the student will not find on the annexed diagram; namely, that in which the second finger is moved *back* on the finger-board to command F sharp, B, E, or A, leaving the first finger free to execute any rapid fingering of the sharp G, D, A, or E alternately with the note above, that may be required. This is called the "back shift," and is often needed in the sharp keys in playing chords, and second violin parts and quick passages generally.

STYLE IN FINGERING.

By this time the student will have realized — perhaps slowly, but none the less emphatically — that, just as there are two ways of fingering a chromatic run on the piano-forte, there are several ways in which a passage may be fingered on the violin, according to the string played upon; and from this discovery, by attentively studying music marked by masters, will spring another, — namely, that there are certain distinct styles or schools of fingering. It is impossible to advocate one style more strongly than another. We inherit all the labors and studies of the past.

That which the early masters had to grope after, we have carelessly thrown at our feet, and can use the knowledge or reject it as we please.

THE MOVEMENT OF THE THUMB IN SHIFTING.

In moving up to the very high positions the thumb of the left hand must be gradually brought under the neck of the violin as the hand is stretched farther over the finger-board; and in playing above the finger-board, or even near its top on the back strings, the thumb must leave the neck of the violin altogether, and rest on the ribs. The neck is easily regained as the hand returns to the lower positions on the shift. I lately saw a good player, and a teacher of some eminence, perform several difficult solos in public without this gradual sliding of the thumb down under the neck. On the high positions the neck of the violin was therefore sunk in the fork of the thumb, and the contortions necessary to command the upper notes must have cost him exquisite torture.

TO SHIFT BY THE WRIST.

The *real* difficulty of shifting is the bringing back of the hand to the first position. For this purpose, as noticed in Chapter V., *the shoulder should never be used.* The only correct and graceful method is to do it with a quick jerk of the wrist. To bring forward the left shoulder is an ungainly contortion almost painful to behold, and certainly quite unnecessary. To acquire facility in shifting back by the wrist it is only necessary to study carefully the movements of which this graceful feat consists. These movements are actually so quick that the eye can scarcely follow them when the feat is performed in the ordinary course of a piece of music. Supposing the student is on the third position,—and all the difficulty lies in getting from that to the first,—let him first grip the violin with moderate firmness on the collar-bone with his chin, then allow his wrist to slide up on the ribs of the violin till the palm of his hand covers the under side of the neck of the violin from the ribs to the nut, being careful, at first, to have no finger on the strings. He will then find that, as soon as the palm of his hand lies on the neck of the violin, his first finger is down at the bottom of the finger-board close to the nut. Let him hold the violin lightly there between first finger and thumb, and then right his hand by throwing out the wrist with a smart jerk into the usual position, and the feat is done. A little practice will perfect him in the movement till, through time, even with a finger on the string, he will be able to make a sweep from the very top of the finger-board to the bottom, without using the shoulder, and with an ease and neatness which will astonish himself. When this dexterity has been attained, the various motions — that is, the sliding-up of the palm and the outward jerk of the wrist — are so swift as to be scarcely discernible.

CHAPTER IX.

ECCENTRICITIES IN BOWING.—THE CURIOUS BOWING OF SCOTTISH STRATHSPEYS ANALYZED AND EXPLAINED.

SCOTTISH music — and more especially that which is not composed as vocal music — defies all rule. Any one with theories of harmony very badly on the brain, and wishing to be driven frantic, need only listen to some of our best Scottish dancing tunes, in which not only consecutive fifths, but consecutive every thing else, are coolly introduced by the melody suddenly in the most eccentric fashion, sinking one note, and repeating the first phrase in that new key, as in "Hobble Jenny" strathspey, Example No. 1; or, as abruptly jumping up one note,

Example No. 1.

Example No. 2.

and repeating the phrase in that new key, as in the "Bob of Fettercairn" reel, Example No. 2. The secret of this idiosyncrasy, I believe, is that the most ancient of these tunes were composed for that primitive and very imperfect instrument, the Scottish bagpipes. The music thus adapted to that instrument became the foundation of a peculiar school of compositions, the writers of which imported all the eccentricities of that school into the music they invented, even when that music was intended for the violin as well as the bagpipes. The bagpipes may perish off the face of the earth, and be heard of no more; but its spirit will haunt purely Scottish and Irish music through all time. How inseparably wedded this music is to the bagpipes and violin is seen the moment we attempt to render genuine Scottish strathspeys or reels upon any other instrument. The whole spirit of the music is gone, swift as the vanishing of Aladdin's palace at the enchanter's command. Strathspeys and reels played on the piano-forte are as ridiculous as would be one of De Beriot's airs varied performed upon a tin whistle. A flute only slobbers them; and a cornopean stumps along through them, like a wooden-legged man trying desperately to keep pace with an agile and graceful runner.

As the goundwork and effect of much of that music is eccentric, so is the bowing by which it is produced. The first thing which strikes the thoughtful violin student when he turns to Scottish strathspeys and reels is, that there is a peculiar laziness, as he would imagine, about the style in which they are bowed, while at the same time the sharpness of the effect is keener than that in any other species of dance music. To hear a reel or strathspey properly played is almost certainly to have the toes set a-tingling for the dance. Yet in the latter music it is no uncommon thing for quite a string of notes to be linked on to one bow, while in reels it is an exceptional case where the notes are not played two slurred and two bowed alternately. The ring, or spirit, or "birr" of the music — which every Scotchman seems to imbibe with the air he breathes — has, no doubt, a good deal to do with the effect; but the bowing has more. The secret of the peculiar laziness I have alluded to — and I can find no better word to described the bowing — is, I believe, that formerly this music formed almost the only music of the ball-room. In those days there was a great deal of spirit in the dancing, including whiskey; and little mercy was shown to the poor fiddlers, who were often kept tearing away at this heavy music for twelve hours at a stretch. Little wonder, then, that they discovered the easiest ways of producing the desired effect, and, having found them, adhered to them most religiously; laying down as a law to all who followed, that that and no other was *the style* in which the music must be played. An awkward crossing from one string to that above or below gave them no concern. To play both notes clean and distinct would have given them an amount of labor which their wearied and paralyzed fingers would surely have refused to execute. They therefore solved the difficulty by coolly sounding both strings together, and gravely rattling on to the next passage. (See Example No. 3, second line.) In like manner they found that all notes *driven,* like the first note in the second bar of "Deeside" strathspey, Example No. 2, given below, could, with but a slight sacrifice of the rhythm, and no loss to the sharpness, be caught at the tip of the bow with a slight jerk of the wrist, off the preceding or leading note, instead of giving it a down bow to itself, and they adopted the plan without hesitation. This catching of the driven note is one of the most striking peculiarities of the Scottish strathspey. I never yet saw it explained in print. Nay, I have met dozens of strathspey players who could do it, but who could not tell how it was done, and so were absolutely unable to impart the secret to another.

No. 1.

No. 2.

No. 3.

If it is difficult to explain this trick of style orally, and with the violin in your hand, it is still more so to do it in print; but I will here attempt the task, convinced that in so doing I will be benefiting many a puzzled learner, and as certain that, though I may not make the thing clear to all, I am giving the real solution of the mystery. In Example No. 1 the student has an easy and intelligible phrase. He has dotted notes, played in the usual manner; that is, with one bow to each two notes, the short note being caught off the first with a slight jerk of the wrist, just as a crotchet and quaver are played in an Irish jig. So far all is plain sailing, as this kind of bowing is given in every exercise book, and is used in jigs, marches, strathspeys, and many other kinds of music. Even the up bow given in Example No. 2 need not puzzle the student much, as it is easy to push on the bow till the three notes are played, and then make up for the loss of bow by drawing the hair more quickly over the next two, to get back to the upper part of the bow. It is, as I have already noticed, the *driven* notes which puzzle most; and to put their peculiarity of bowing lucidly before the student's eye, and through that impress it on his mind, I have designed the Exercises Nos. 4, 5, and 6.

STUMPIE.—Strathspey, 2nd Part.

In Example No. 4 is given a phrase from "Stumpie" strathspey as it is usually written or printed. The novice, seeing the notes for the first time, would apply the ordinary rules of bowing to the passage, and give the first note, D, an up bow; and the second, or driven note, a down bow; and the third, the open string E, an up bow. But mark what would be the result. The next two notes, dotted in the ordinary manner, would get one down bow to the two; and then would come an insuperable obstacle,—the playing of a driven note with an up bow. Indeed the ordinary rules of bowing could not be continued through many bars of any strathspey without hopelessly enmeshing the student in difficulties. Let him now turn to Example No. 5, and study closely the bowing as there marked. Although there is a slur over the first bar connecting the first two notes, it must not be thought that this implies the smoothness which a slur usually represents. At the end of the slur is a dot to show that the note is to be picked off sharply with a jerk of the wrist when the bow has passed across the string to near its point. The moment this note is sounded, the bow is reversed for the open string note, E, moving the bow rather more quickly across the string, so that a long sweep may be left for the next down bow, which has three notes linked on to it. The next note with the dot over it, D, is caught at the top of the bow with the same peculiar jerk of the wrist, which is really only another form of that used in Example No. 1, and so the tune proceeds. Now, I have shown that our forerunners in violin-playing, in hitting upon this bowing as peculiar and easy of execution as it is inspiriting in its effect, actually discovered the only mode by which the music could be performed without landing the player in worse difficulties than those thus ingeniously surmounted. But the peculiar method, which has now become so inseparably wedded to the music as to be considered one of its constituent parts, was not a complete gain. If the student will get a good strathspey player to rattle through the second part of "Stumpie,"—which he will do by bowing it exactly as I have marked it, and will listen attentively,—he will find that there is a palpable sacrifice of the rhythm of the melody. What that effect is, I have tried to visibly represent in Example No. 6; but I may say that the representation there given would be nearer the real effect if the first bar were driven down through the middle of the second note, C, and all the other bars in the line were helped forward in like manner into the middle of the note behind which I have placed them. An attentive examination of the example will possibly call forth the exclamation, "Surely, there is something wrong in that way of bringing the note forward before the bar, or even on to it!" but, as I said in starting, Scottish music is amenable to no rule whatever. That *is*, undoubtedly, the effect produced; but whether it is wrong or right depends upon the stand-point from which we regard it. It is part of the music, bone of its bone and flesh of its flesh; and, just as we are *forced* to accept without question the consecutive fifths already noticed,—for no other harmony is possible,—so must we accept the peculiar effect of these driven notes. It is this trick of style which so staggers and appals foreign or even English violinists. They cannot give even the feeblest imitation of the effect, though possibly masters of the instrument in every other sense, and, when their most strenuous efforts only induce a smile from the experienced listener, sometimes lose temper, and innocently insist that they are playing the music as it is written. The student who masters this bowing is a long distance on the way to becoming a good strathspey player. He has crossed a magic Rubicon, beyond which progress is rapid and easy.

It is often said, and with perfect truth, that no two strathspey players play the same tune exactly alike; each one scraping away according to his own sweet will. In Example No. 3 I have given first the opening bars of the "Duchess of Gordon's" strathspey as they are written, and then the same notes as I heard them rendered by a first-rate Aberdeen strathspey player. It is clear that when masters of the style take such liberties, no definite rule can be given for playing the tunes; but, just as while there are several ways in which a passage might be fingered, there are general rules for guidance in all cases: so in stratshspey playing there are peculiarities which must be mastered and practised by all, no matter what liberties they may take with the melody. Those bowings which I have here analyzed are the foremost among these pecularities. Most of the others are amenable to ordinary rules.

THE LONG BOW FOR THE STRATHSPEY.

I may say, however, that it is a mistake to suppose that only a short, twiddling bow should be used in strathspey playing. The best players use the full sweep of the bow, always catching the driven notes in the manner I have described, even when two couples of these occur in succession. Occasionally a strathspey is agreeably varied by a run in triplets.

PLAYING TRIPLETS.

These triplets must be played entirely with the upper half of the bow, giving a bow to each quaver, and *never slurring the three*. A great many of these triplets are marked with slurs, — particularly in old music, — not because they were meant to be slurred, but because the old fashion was to so indicate a triplet introduced into a common-time tune, with the addition of a figure 3 beneath the slur.

REEL PLAYING.

In playing reels the same precaution must be observed, *only the upper half of the bow being used*. A great deal of the spirit of a reel is given by accenting strongly the first and third beat of the bar, as in Example No. 7 ("Rachel Rae"); and also by slurring and bowing alternately every two notes, as in Example No. 8 ("Fife Hunt"). Some reels, however, with much crossing of the strings, must have a bow to each note, as, for instance, the third complete bar in "The Deil among the Tailors." The reel should be practised rather slow at first, until every note can be sounded clear and smooth, when the proper speed can easily be given.

THE BOWING OF HORNPIPES, NEWCASTLE STYLE.

In a chapter devoted to peculiar dance music and eccentric bowing, it would be wrong to omit mention of the Newcastle style of bowing hornpipes. The Newcastle hornpipe is a slower composition than the sailor's, and designed chiefly for clog-dancing. Like the strathspey, it is often agreeably varied by triplets, which are bowed and not slurred, and when properly played has a good deal of the two following styles of bowing:—

No. 1. *Moderato.*

No. 2.

Example No. 1 presents no great difficulty till the last note in the second last bar is reached. This note, E, is bowed with a jerk of the wrist, and not slurred over the bar like the others. When the student has mastered that trick, he will find the bowing of Example No. 2 not so stupendously difficult. This is sometimes called the "back bow" from the bow being moved back instead of forward. There are two kinds of "back bowing," that in Example No. 2 being the most difficult. This bowing presents the peculiarity that it cannot be well played slow; that is, the effect is then all but lost to the ear, and the learner of course cannot at first play it fast. The other form of the "back bow" is that alluded to and exemplified in Spohr's 21st and 31st exercises, and is used in slow, quiet music for dotted notes, which are not wished so sharp and crisp as those caught up in the usual way, two to each bow. This bowing of Spohr's, though it has never a graceful appearance to the eye, is often required when the bow needs righting, and also, as above noted, in particular kinds of music, such as *adagios* and *andantes*, and presents no great difficulty to the learner. It is the rapid form of the "back bow" which staggers most players. To master it the student must play with the *upper third part* of the bow only, playing the leading notes, — namely, those immediately before the bar, with an inversion of the rules of bowing, — that is, with a strongly accented down bow. The first note in the bar is then played with an up bow, the short note after it being then crisply caught with a quick down stroke. It must be played vigorously and with great spirit. No written description can convey any idea of the neat sprightliness of this style of bowing; and it is absolutely necessary that every violin-player should master it, not for hornpipes alone, but for every kind of music which has groups of very quick dotted notes, such as, for instance, the second part of the "Market Chorus" in "Masaniello," and dozens of other passages which will readily occur to the student.

THE BOWING OF IRISH JIGS.

The rules for the bowing of strathspeys and reels may be applied to most of the peculiarities of Irish jigs and reels; the crotchet and quaver in the jig being played like an ordinary dotted note of two notes to the bow, except in some cases where a specially strong and distinct accent is wished, when the crotchet is played with a strong down bow, and the quaver with a light up stroke.

THE BOWING OF IRISH REELS.

The alternate slurring and bowing of every two notes in Scotch reels is also applicable to Irish reels. There is, however, a peculiar swing in the Irish reel, and the notes are sometimes dotted: so on the whole it ought to be played somewhat slower than its Scottish brother.

HARMONIZED STRATHSPEYS.

It is no uncommon thing now-a-days to hear selections of strathspeys and reels performed by an orchestra upon the platform; but the very fact that the toes and heels of the audience are generally set a-dancing and stamping seems to be a proof that this music is there clearly out of its proper place, which is the ball-room. But, if this music is to be given thus, there is no reason why it should not be given in purity. A number of second violins or violas drumming away at chords, with a clarionet, flute, or cornet tooting in occasionally with their unwelcome notes, is as outrageous as daubing the lily with paint. Originally in these tunes the bass was supplied by the drones of the bagpipes. Then the violoncello took its place. It had to stop there. From the primitive simplicity of the melodies there was and could be room for no other harmony; and to add a second violin part is only to show ignorance, and an absence of that subtle insight which must regulate all arrangements of purely national music.

And what of all this? Is the playing of strathspeys and reels and clog hornpipes high art? Well, it cannot exactly be called high art; but it is at least a wonderful art. It is an important branch of violin-playing, and one of which every Scottish violinist ought to blush not to be master. Many look to it as the acme of their ambition; others look higher,—a long way. It is often said, and with truth, that much strathspey playing unfits the player for the artistic performance of any other kind of music; and it is notorious that most of the great strathspey players have been good at nothing else. But the same may be said of any kind of music which is over-practised, whether exercises, classical music, dance music, or solos. The student who wishes to excel must practise *every kind of music*,—make frequent changes even in his exercise books, and the studies he labors at in these books; and he who adopts this practice will receive much real benefit by at least mastering the peculiar bowings here explained.

CHAPTER X.

THE GRACES OF SOLO PLAYING.

ANY tune may be made a solo. It all depends upon how it is arranged and played. The student will realize the truth of this statement before he is long at the instrument. He will hear the commonest or most trifling melody taken up by a masterly player, and made perfectly entrancing by the manner in which it is articulated. To play a solo well, then, is to be master of all that is fine and subtle and delicate in the art of violin-playing. The glassy slide; the ringing, open shake; the weird tremola, or close shake; the pearly staccato bow; the vocal sweep of the fingers from one position to another; the brilliant and flutelike harmonic; the wailing double stopping, and all the intricacies of exceptional fingering, come here into full play.

STYLE AND FINGERING IN SOLO PLAYING.

The positions and fingering adopted by a solo player depend a good deal upon the qualities of his instrument. Every violin has its strong and its weak points; and the skilful player adopts a fingering and style which will bring the beauties of his instrument into prominence, and keep the defects in the background. For instance, any one having a violin with a particularly fine-toned third string, and wishing to play the *thema* of the fantasia on "Alice," given below in Example No. 2, would adopt the fingering and positions given below the line; while one whose second string was particularly good, and the third feeble, or stumpy and poor would probably adopt that given above the line. Again, no two players, even though trained under the same master, adopt the same *style* of playing. One will become a player all fire and fury, fond of strong effects, "bitten" notes, *tremola* playing, and noise and astonishment generally; another will adopt smoothness and sweetness as his ideal, and will probably lose tone and strength without a sigh, that he may develop these qualities; another will be all tricks and show, and tinsel-like effects. The playing, indeed, will, to a certain extent par-

No. 1.

No. 2.

No. 3.

No. 4.

No. 5.

take of the nature of the player, just as in literature the inner nature of an author is bound sooner or later to appear in his works. Therefore it will not do for us to say this style or that style is right or wrong. We can only thank the Creator of all for the infinite variety with which he has crowned his work for our blessing, and, looking on all as good, select that style to which we are most strongly drawn by our powers and conceptions, at best but limited.

THE SLIDE.

The slide is a smooth gliding of the finger in use up to a note above, generally an harmonic, as given in the first bar of Example No. 1. Another style of the slide, a kind of combination of Spohr's style of shifting and the slide proper, which I have never seen noticed in any book, but have found very effective, is given in Example No. 3. The finger in use is slid up on the string any distance till the disengaged fourth finger is nearly above the harmonic to be played, when the little finger is brought down lightly on the harmonic. This has a surprisingly smooth and sweet, and at the same time vocal, effect. Another example of the slide, though a somewhat dangerous one to indulge in, will be found in the last bar of Example No. 2. There is no slide which is more effective than this when properly executed, and it is not uncommon for a succession of such slides to be executed with one finger, as in Example No. 5; but there is always a danger of false intonation. Soloists who indulge much in it, I have noticed, often play out of tune. This slide therefore must be used with great discrimination, and religiously avoided when there is the slightest danger of slipping or bad stopping. Another very effective slide, and a much surer one to use, is—in playing two notes such as those in the last bar of Example No. 5, supposing the shake were absent—to put the second finger firmly down in its place, slip the first finger as close up behind it as it will go, then lift the second, and slowly draw back the first on the string till it reaches D natural, slurring the whole on to one bow. This is very effective when finished off with a nicely swelled close shake on the D.

THE OPEN SHAKE.

The open shake is a rapid repetition of the note above alternately with that marked; and the best directions for acquiring it are those given by Spohr,—to raise the finger as high as possible from the string at every beat of the shake, and not to attempt to do a fast shake all at once. If rapidity be aimed at too early the shake will always be weak and feeble, the finger, as Spohr expresses it, appearing to get lamed before the shake is half finished. Sometimes a succession of running shakes are introduced for one finger, as in Example No. 5, when the change in position between each must be taken with great exactness and rapidity. An even more difficult form is that in which the shake is on every note, and no interruption of the beats is allowed during the shifting. Nos. 18, 19, 20, and 21 in Kreutzer's "Studies" are the best exercises I know of for strengthening the fingers for the long and short open shake. More especially are they to be diligently practised, as they give great strength and firmness to the fourth finger, which is shorter and—in violin-playing at least—weaker than any of the others.

THE CLOSE SHAKE.

The close shake is a slight deviation from true to false intonation, rapidly repeated, by causing the finger to rise and fall on the string without actually quitting it. It is a most effective ally of the solo player; but it is one which is greatly abused, and often introduced where it has no right to appear. Indeed, with some solo players it appears impossible to play a clear, steady, pure note, without the perpetual *tremola* coming in like an evil spirit or haunting ghost to mar its beauty. To acquire the close shake the first thing to be studied is to have the whole hand free of the neck or ribs of the violin, except at those parts where it is touched by the fleshy part of the thumb upon which it rests, and the point of the finger in use. A high nut and bridge make the close shake much easier by presenting a more marked difference of false and true stopping in the straight and depressed string. A very good note for the novice to begin with is D on the second string, with the hand advanced to the third position. Place the first finger on the string, let the hand be otherwise loose and free, and then cause such a trembling motion to run along the wrist and finger as shall make the finger-point rise and fall on the string without actually quitting it. Be sure to have no other finger pressing on the string but that used for stopping the note which is being quivered on. In ordinary playing it is often an advantage to keep down the fingers behind that which is being used, but it is not so in performing the close shake. With beginners the feat is sometimes easier with a down bow than with the up stroke, and by playing with the bow closer to the bridge, the hair pressed steadily on the string, and the tone full and strong. Even if only a few slow waves in the tone are accomplished at first the groundwork of success is laid just as progress in the mastering of the open shake is not to be judged by the rapidity of the beat. When the close shake on D is mastered, the hand may be brought down to the first position, and a shake on B with the same finger be tried. If the student finds any difficulty here owing to the first finger getting locked or pressed against the neck of the violin instead of being perfectly loose and free, except where the point presses on the string, he may at first allow the wrist to approach the bottom of the ribs of the violin, and, resting the instrument lightly between that and the thumb, execute the close shake on the B, or any other note he requires thus ornamented. A little practice will soon enable him to master the difficulty. The only danger is, that when he has acquired this grace he will abuse it by bringing it in everywhere in his solos. Like the beats in the open shake the quiverings are often begun slow in a long note, and gradually increased in rapidity, and *vice versa;* and a fine effect may be introduced by this gradual increasing and diminishing of the quiverings in playing a note swelled and diminished. The close shake like the staccato bow is much more easily mastered by some than others. A light hand and loose joints are a great help; but, whatever the nature of the hand, the great indispensable is to have the left hand as free as possible of contact with the violin.

THE SWELL.

The power to swell and diminish the tone by graduating the pressure of the first finger on the stick of the bow, as explained on page 47, is a much more valuable and legitimate aid to art than the close shake, and one which *can never be abused;* yet with many accomplished players it is a grace unknown. The student will get more real benefit from half an hour's practice at that than from twenty devoted to the close shake.

THE STACCATO BOW.

The staccato bow is that delicate succession of short strokes in one direction which enables a performer to give a run of twenty-five or more distinctly detached notes with one bow. It is a beautiful and graceful accomplishment, and well worth all the slow study and practice by which alone it can be mastered. Spohr gives several exercises for the staccato bow; but the best I have seen is to be found on pages 4 and 5 of Kreutzer's "Studies," already mentioned. Another easy and beautiful study for this bowing is Variation No. 2 in De Beriot's "Third Air Varied." Those given on pages 59 and 60 of Saint Jacome's edition of Auguste Marque's "Method" are also excellent. There is also a study of no special excellence in Loder. The first note in each run given in these studies is to be played with a strongly accented down bow, which *ends only at the extreme point of the bow*, and gives a spring to the bow when it is reversed for the up stroke, which enables the performer to pick out every note of the run, clean and smooth, with a slight pressure of the first finger on the stick, till the run is finished, when the bow is captured and held fast by a strongly accented note played in the same direction or a fresh down bow, which in turn often gives the starting spring for another staccato bow. All writers agree that the staccato bow must be practised very slowly and distinctly at first, and, as only the upper half of the bow can be used effectively for the accomplishment, it follows that a beginner can execute only a short run of six or eight notes before he finds himself crossing the magic Rubicon, the centre of the bow, beyond which the bow appears to get in a manner overbalanced, and loses its beauty and power in staccato. The whole width of the hair touches the string at each note, no matter how long the run, and only the extreme outer edge of the hair when the bow rises from the performance of each note. The fact that the hair must not once quit the string during the entire performance of the staccato run cannot be too strongly impressed upon the student. This is the first great essential towards mastery of the bowing; and three others as important are, that the first and last notes of the run be strongly accented, that only the upper half of the bow be used, and that the runs be played slowly at first. As I have met many advanced players who had either but a confused idea of what constitutes the real staccato bow, or were too careless or indolent to acquire the proper style, I may here distinctly state that a mere stutter of the bow on the string, however showily executed, is *not* the staccato bow, and is quite incapable of producing, in a tone worth listening to, a string of smooth, clean, pearly notes. Spohr says that many acquire this delightful grace of art without an effort, while others, labor as they may, never get it to satisfaction; and the secret of this fact

I believe to be that those who do thus acquire it with ease have the bow particularly well balanced and correctly held in every particular before they begin the study. There must not be the slightest slope on the string or movement of the violin during the performance of the feat; and the student who soonest learns to economize the amount of hair used for each note will soonest master this difficult bowing. In the slow study which precedes perfection in this art the student should aim at a *distinct and clear articulation* of each note, rather than at a rapid increase in the number of notes he can execute before reaching the middle of the bow, When the up stroke of the staccato bow is mastered, the down stroke may be studied, still using only the upper half of the bow. The downward staccato bow has never the same brightness and elasticity as the up stroke; but both are imperatively called for in some compositions, as, for instance, the staccato variation in De Beriot's "Seventh Air Varied."

THE BASTARD STACCATO BOW.

There is, besides the delightful and pearly bowing I have here described and explained, a bastard staccato bow, which is often used in orchestral and other music where great lightness and fairy-like delicacy is required in a rapid repetition of one note, such as those in the Rondo from "William Tell." This is very easy of accomplishment, and is simply a light stutter of the bow on the string, up or down stroke, the upper part alone being used in the bowing. The effect is surprisingly neat and pretty, especially when the bowing is executed by a dozen or so of first violins at once.

THE BITING STACCATO BOW.

A third kind of staccato bow is used for a succession of strongly marked quavers, and executed by stopping any part of the bow, generally the lower part, on the string, to allow it to "grip," and then biting out the note, as it were, and so continuing to bite out each note till the phrase is finished. This "biting out" of the notes, however, is a dangerously seductive style of bowing, and apt to degenerate into a pernicious habit, detrimental to all fine and *legato* playing. I notice these two last styles of bowing principally, that they may not be confounded with the staccato bow proper, to which they have no affinity or relation either in effect or the manner in which they are mastered.

HARMONIC PLAYING.

Harmonics are a kind of *falsetto* notes which arise from a string when it vibrates from two sides of a node at once. Subjoined I have given a complete list of the natural harmonics which arise from the strings of the violin, and the exact spot on which they are found. To produce them clearly the bow must be turned rather more on its outer edge than usual, and drawn with great steadiness and some lightness across the string, the weight of the bow being taken from the string by a slight pressure of the little finger on the stick, and the finger used for stopping the note being only laid lightly on the string, and not pressed close to the finger-board as usual.

Table of the Natural Harmonics arising from the Strings of the Violin.

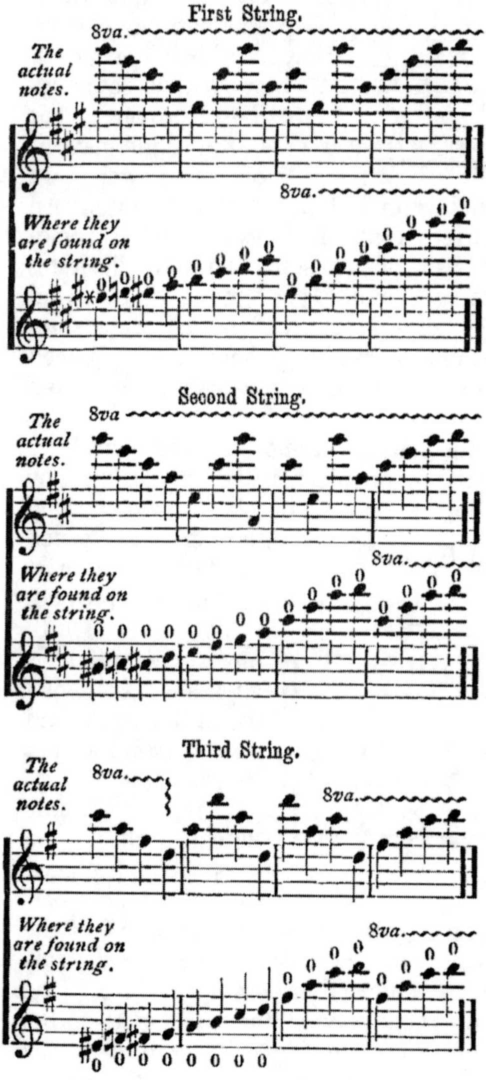

The study of harmonics is interesting in more ways than one. If the student will pick out the natural harmonics of any string as here given and transfer them to the piano, he will find, if he understands a little har-

Fourth String.

The note given first on each string is to be played only a quarter of a tone sharp.

mony, that the notes form the constituent parts of the chord of the major seventh — or, in sol-fa language, the "soh-te-ray-fah" chord — upon which all harmony, however wild, or weird, or rich, is sounded, thus proving that those combinations of sound which we call harmony are not an invention, but a part of nature. An Æolian harp, with the strings tuned in unison, which I sometimes fasten under the sash of my study window, illustrates this fact in a very pleasing manner; performing, as the wind rises and falls, the most fairy-like successions and inversions and combinations of this chord, entirely in harmonics. Indeed the name of this instrument ought to be, not Æolian harp, but harmonicon.

As a supplement to the natural harmonics Example No. 2 will show how an artificial harmonic may be made on any string and in any position, the lower, or black note, showing the spot on which the first finger must be firmly pressed, while the fourth finger, as usual, is allowed to lightly touch the string and no more on the spot indicated by the upper note. A fine flutelike effect can thus be introduced into a variation, particularly on the fourth string; but, if the rounding-off of the notes is not particularly desired, the scale may be played partly with natural harmonics, as indicated in Example No. 3. The scale will be found in the same way on the same spots on the other strings, only a fifth or more higher, according to the string played upon. There is sometimes a slight difficulty in

Example of Artificial Harmonics.

Fourth String.

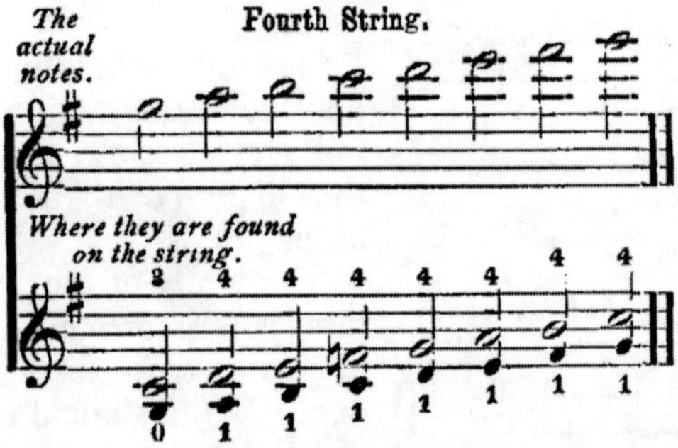

getting the artificial harmonics to ring out clearly: indeed they occasionally "miss fire" altogether. If this should occur with any particular note, it may generally be remedied by playing with the fourth finger held slightly sharp of its position on the string.

Example of Natural and Artificial Harmonics combined.

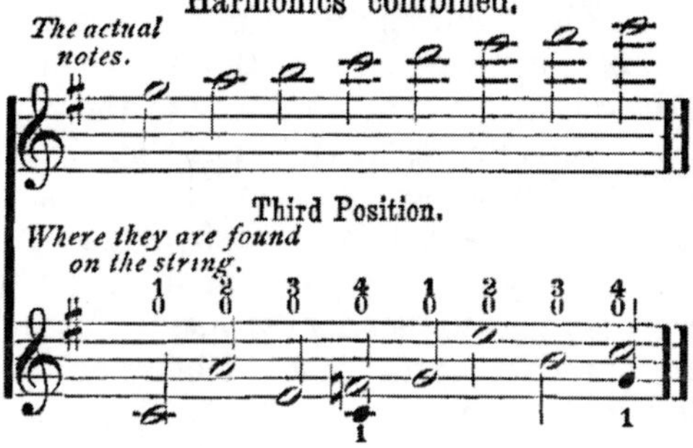

Spohr vigorously denounces the use of harmonics in this extended sense; but, before we can understand the headlong condemnation, we must consider the period at which his work was written. Paganini, the most astounding and meteoric genius who ever conjured music from the violin, had just swept across the musical world, and everywhere there was being heard nothing but the most diligent imitation of his impassioned style and eccentric tricks. Close shaking on every note; monochord playing; pizzicatos, and, above all, harmonics, were the rage or fashion of the day; and it seemed as if a pure and classic style was a thing of the past. To remedy this state of things Spohr—himself the very antipodes of the towering, hot-blooded Italian wizard—set himself to denounce wholesale the tricks by which it was mistakenly supposed Paganini had made his name, just as it is the fashion to denounce as a mere trick the curious bad spelling of Artemus Ward, and entirely overlook the genius in character-painting, and the sly satire and subtle wit which underlies the whole. A critique written under such circumstances and by such a man as Spohr could scarcely be sound in every particular; and in point of fact the decision has long been overturned and ignored by, not the very highest of players, certainly, but a very high class of composers and performers; and harmonics are now properly looked upon as a brilliant and indispensable addition to the ornaments of solo playing. Spohr says that artificial harmonics can only be produced on thin strings; but in saying so he undoubtedly said the thing which is not. Harmonics, artificial or natural, if they are fingered and bowed properly, will ring out clear as a bell and soft and glassy as a flute on any kind of string, thick or thin. Harmonics do not excite wonder alone. They can be made to stir a deep feeling in the breast,—a sense of breathless interest and deep pleasure, mingled with a sigh that the performance has ended so soon. The advanced student ought never to rest till he has mastered their performance.

THE PLAYING OF CHORDS.

Double stopping, or the playing of chords, is one of the most attractive graces of solo playing. When with the double stopping is combined a judicious and artistic rendering of the close shake, there is produced a deep *wailing* effect,—a thrilling intensity of pathos of which the listener feels he can never drink in enough. To play chords well,—that is, perfectly in tune,—though four notes should be required at once, requires a special ability. It is useless to say that the student's "ear" must tell him when he is right, and practice do the rest. I know an eminent professor of music whose "ear" is finically acute, and who cannot play or hear played a single note in the slightest degree false without instantly detecting the error, yet who, the moment he begins playing chords on the violin, plays them atrociously out of tune; and his case is but one out of thousands. Spohr notices this fact, and advises that the pupil be forced *from the first* to play them perfectly in tune; but no fixed rule or advice will apply to this defect. The student can only be warned that such a rock ahead is in the way, and be left to escape as best he can. In playing second violin, or any part requiring the use of chords, in a warm room, the strings often relax long before it is possible to retune; and then the player's ear must remedy the defect, his fingers being placed slightly sharp on the strings which are wrong. Sometimes in a solo a chord of two notes is played with an open shake upon both notes, which is called a DOUBLE SHAKE,—a grace as surprisingly delightful to the ear as it is difficult of performance.

PLAYING ARPEGGIOS.

Arpeggios are simply chords played with their constituent notes detached into runs. As they are most often played with a slur to the down bow and a staccato bow for the up stroke, they require a firm wrist and well-balanced bow, rather tight in the hair, as well as great accuracy in the stopping of the notes of the chord. It is a good plan to strongly accent the down bow at the lowest portion of the chord, and then let it rise with a spring to execute the back stroke or succession of strokes. In reading arpeggios, chords, and difficult music generally, a knowledge of harmony will be found of great assistance, as whole phrases and long runs extending over many bars may then be read at a glance, being recognized as merely a *spread-out* form of a certain chord or progression in harmony. This is particularly the case in playing overtures, concertos, and classical music generally, especially when reading "at sight."

PIZZICATO PLAYING.

Pizzicatos are in solos generally condemned as mere trick-playing. They are executed with the fourth, or any other convenient finger of the left hand, and sometimes, when in chords of four notes, by twitching the strings with the second finger of the right hand, the bow being held the while between the first and thumb, or with the thumb resting on the front edge of the finger-board near the top, the bow resting in the fork, and the notes sounded by being twitched neatly with the first finger of the right hand. Pizzicatos excite the wonder of the listener, but never move the feelings: therefore to them must be relegated the very lowest position in the subtle arts of solo playing.

SPOHR'S STYLE OF SHIFTING.

In Example No. 4, page 77, I have given a specimen of Spohr's masterly style of shifting with absolute certainty any distance up or down the string. In making this sweep the first finger is swiftly advanced on the string till it reaches that position on which the note required is immediately under the fourth finger, which, the moment that position is reached, must be brought slap down on the note. The same method is observed in coming down the string, the finger immediately below that to be used being drawn back till it reaches the note immediately below that required, when the proper finger is at once used. In the examples the guiding note in the sweep is indicated by a smaller note. Another form of the same trick, but here used to give a more vocal effect to the note following, will be seen in the second and third complete bars of Example No. 1, and in the third bar of No. 2. This is a powerful grace of art in the hands of all masters of the instrument, especially in *andante* and *adagio* movements. It is this trick, combined with the close shake, which so often elicits the remark, "He fairly made the instrument *speak*." The student therefore should practise it diligently, using it discreetly, and with that art which conceals art.

CHAPTER XI.

THE SOLO DESCRIBED.

I HAVE now noticed in brief the chief graces of style required by the solo player, and may now describe the solo itself. A solo generally consists of an introduction more or less florid, an air with variations, and a stirring coda, or finale. A fantasia is a somewhat similar composition: but in this species of solo rather more latitude is allowed the composer, who may introduce more airs than one, varied or not, as strikes his taste; and the fantasia may therefore be considered a more ambitious effort than any mere air varied. Supposing the student to begin with the simple solo, he will give the introduction with all the variety of tone, grace of expression, and florid art of which he is master, the introduction taking the same place in the solo which the introduction does in a speech, in which the orator, by some happy hit, or personal allusion, or graceful compliment, gets himself entirely into the sympathies of his audience before once touching on the business proper to his speech. This done, he will probably have a few bars' rest to quietly tune any of the strings which may have relaxed, or wipe his violin, or slacken or tighten the hair of his bow, as the *thema* may require, during which the piano-forte will have a short symphony. This over, he will play the *thema*, or air, in all its purity and simplicity, aiming at a reading as closely allied as possible to the singing of a song by a fine soprano voice. If the air be that of a well-known song, it is an excellent plan to learn off at least one verse of the words, that every expression and line of thought may be faithfully followed in his playing. The variations will then follow, particular care being taken that all that is wished neat, or sprightly, or ringing in brilliance shall be executed with the upper half or the upper third part of the bow, and all that is crisp and noisy with the lower part. The *finale*, which is generally an allegro and double forte, may be executed with the middle third part of the bow, the finishing chords of the coda being given with long down bows, swiftly flashed, and taken from the string with a startling crispness at each chord.

THE SELECTION OF SOLOS.

In studying high-class music, such as sonatas, fantasias, or concertos, it is well for the player to select solos or studies considerably beyond his powers. The first look at a new solo or selection generally staggers or overawes the student. The first trial of the various movements on his instrument does worse: it fills his heart with despair, and induces some such remarks as, "Why did I buy the thing? I'll never be able to play that, — never!". After a little, however, by repeated trials, he finds that the difficulties become familiar to the eye, and seem less appalling to the fingers. One by one the movements are mastered, till the difficulties are reduced to perhaps half a dozen particular phrases in different parts of the solo. These hold out against all his efforts, as if determined to conquer him. Yet it is they which must be conquered; and to do so they must be attacked, like outnumbering forces in war, singly. Each of the passages must be marked out from the rest of the solo, and played, and played by itself for fifty times in succession if necessary, slowly at first, till they also yield to the performer. Tried then, in their proper place in the solo, their beauty or brilliance is at once realized, and the student is at liberty to go on conquering and to conquer with more difficult pieces.

SOLO PLAYING FROM MEMORY.

If the student has a good memory, he ought to learn his solos off. The music-stand is always a source of stiffness and discomfort on the platform; and when able to dispense with that, and with having his eye rigidly fixed on the music, the performer is more able to attend to that perfect grace and freedom of style which is inseparable from a thoroughly pleasing delivery of violin music. In practising a solo it is best to try several ways of fingering before deciding which is most effective; including, as this does, the shifting of the melody from one string on to another, which may give it more effect. In cadenzas and other florid passages a slight addition may sometimes be made to the original composition with great effect, according to the taste and skill of the player.

ORCHESTRAL PLAYING.

Very early the student ought to get into some amateur orchestra, quartet party, or musical society, that he may learn steadiness in time, and how to sink himself and his instrument, and become only a part of the grand whole. In orchestral or quartet playing great steadiness and purity of intonation, great exactness in stopping chords, and strict mental counting of time are the essential qualifications for success. A rather tighter bow is required for orchestral playing than for a solo. When a number of bars are marked silent,—usually by the number being written over a blank bar,—it is safest to count them mentally by always naming the number of the bar counted at the beginning of each: as 1, 2, 3, 4; 2, 2, 3, 4; 3, 2, 3, 4; 4, 2, 3, 4, etc.

QUARTET PLAYING.

In quartet playing proper the melody generally goes the round of the instruments as a solo,—first the leading violin, then the second, then the tenor, and then the violoncello; and during the performance of these solos the remaining instruments, no matter what their grade, or how showy their part, must sink themselves into mere accompanists, anxious only how the soloist may be assisted to show his taste and skill. Indeed, in quartet playing nobody is better than anybody else; and the second violin and tenor, or violoncello, who are too commonly lorded over and snubbed by the leading violin, for once may look around without fear, and dictate and raise themselves to their full height without any one daring to object.

SONATA PLAYING.

As a study for fine solo playing there is nothing so good as the sonata, which is generally not showy but deep; not tricky but truly artistic; not overpoweringly difficult, but nevertheless requiring close study and much critical taste and fine feeling in its execution. All the great masters have excelled in the composition of sonatas. The sonata as a solo requires a discerning audience, and should never be selected when there is not finely developed classical taste in the listeners. A tricky solo, full of nimble pizzicatos and grunting farmyard effects, will often rouse an audience to raptures, when a sonata, however finely articulated, would only be received with ill-suppressed yawns. The sonata is for the chamber concert, the private recital, and, above all, for home study and practice. There is a soul or spirit within it which appears only to the most devoted of its worshippers.

CONCERTO PLAYING.

There is a peculiar individuality about the violin, — a something which makes it stand out from a crowd of instruments as a genius stands out from ordinary men. This peculiarity is found in no other instrument in the same degree; and that fact has induced many of the great composers to exert themselves in the composition of pieces in which the soloist, being accompanied by a full orchestra, brings out this quality to its fullest advantage. These pieces are called concertos. Spohr gives directions and hints as to the performance of the concerto, which will be studied by every violin-player attempting this arduous performance, and says that a *full tone* is the first essential. Some players never try to develop a full tone, even after mastering the difficulties I have pointed out in these chapters; that is, they are content with an ordinary development, never putting the *strongest possible* pressure on the bow with the first finger. If any one will watch Joachim or Madame Neruda, or any of the great players, one of the first things that will strike him will be that at times the hair of the bow seems almost *glued* to the string. This is nothing but the result of a fully developed tone, caused by the strongest possible pressure of the forefinger on the stick of the bow compatible with a smooth and elastic note. Let the student put *tone* before him as an object of attainment, and he will, through time, notice something like the same appearance on his own bow.

THE PERFECTION OF BOWING.

This peculiar cleaving of the hair to the string comes only after years of practice, and may be seen when the tone is not required particularly loud, but only pure and full, or even in the comparatively light bow required for the playing of a succession of clear harmonics. To acquire it there must be a perfect mastery of all the technical details of good bowing; that is, every finger and muscle must have its proper work and no more to do, and do it. The bow must be so perfectly balanced between the forefinger and thumb, with the thumb turned out strongly against the hair, and so deftly supported by the point of the little finger, that it might be pushed or drawn above the violin within a hair's breadth of the string for its whole length without actually touching it. This implies such a command of the stick, that when it is placed upon the string its whole weight could at any moment be taken from the string by a slight touch of the point of the little finger, or the utmost possible pressure be as swiftly applied to it by the first finger. It implies also perfect action of the wrist in support of the action of the fingers, and also a slight raising of the bow from the string at the end of long notes requiring the whole length of the hair. It implies, indeed, many little niceties which cannot be reduced to words, but the effect of which will be recognized the moment this acme of good bowing is attained.

SYSTEMATIC ARRANGEMENT OF STUDIES.

I have now, as clearly and concisely as I can, gone over nearly all that a student needs to learn from his teacher, and in conclusion would advise him to introduce as much variety as possible into his studies by writing out a complete list of all the music in his possession which he thinks worth studying; arranging a different study for each hour at his command for practice, and never letting one hour steal the study allotted to another. This effectually prevents the overlook of much good music which insensibly gets neglected. Lastly, I would say, let him play as *often as he can*, if only for five minutes at a time, especially during the first ten years he is at the instrument. A few minutes in youth are worth many days in after years. The thought, "I have no time," will never dismay the really eager student. He can make time; he can steal the hours from sleep; he can rise early or sit late; he can watch that not a moment that is his own is uselessly frittered away; he can take a thousand opportunities of mingling with musicians more advanced than himself, and improving his powers that another would never dream were his own. Musicians, and more especially violinists, are, with some miserable exceptions, a band of brothers, ever kindly disposed and encouraging to the eager learner; and by deferentially listening to their advice and opinions, and adopting as much of it as experience proves to be sound or suited to the style of playing which he has adopted as his model, the student may be constantly learning and advancing.

When I was a boy I could not afford to pay a teacher for lessons. Though eager to learn, I knew nothing of the various Tutors for the violin which have been written and composed, and, if I had known them by name, could not have bought them; and, if I had had them given me, would not have understood how to use them, as there are dozens of points of detail and necessary instruction upon which all published Tutors are absolutely silent. Had such a work as this been thrown in my way, it would have saved me years of weary struggling and blind groping, and repeated retracing of steps and unlearning of evil habits of style. That thought has been my sole incentive to the penning of these chapters. The work has been done neither for applause, for money, nor for fame. I am convinced that there are hundreds with every natural gift necessary to make them good players who are in as disadvantageous a position as I was, — possibly in some cases more unfortunately situated. Every young lad now-a-days, however poor, can afford to buy a cheap little work like this; and to hundreds who may love the violin as devoutly as I these instructions and directions may prove a lasting boon. Let me therefore hope that, when success has come, — when the instrument is so far mastered as to become a joy in prosperity, a solace in grief or bereavement, a companion in loneliness or neglect, or possibly a means of support in unlooked-for poverty, — the student will think of the nameless writer who, unsolicited, tried to direct him in the right way, and be grateful.

APPENDIX.

ATTITUDE OF THE PERFORMER.

MANY beginners in violin-playing may not see Spohr's work for years after commencing the study, by which time evil habits of holding the instrument or using the bow might be formed. Again, the illustrations given in that great work are not quite correct, as already indicated, and therefore apt to mislead. It is almost impossible for any artist to draw such diagrams correctly *by the eye.* No pictures, as a rule, err more frequently than those introducing violin-players or the violin. I saw a woodcut lately in a good publication in which one infuriated character was pictured smashing a violin. The instrument — which, by the way, had no sound holes — was upraised, the strings were entirely severed and hanging over at each end, and yet the bridge stood erect and firm in its place on the violin! That artist had certainly glue on the brain.

One most important point in proper bowing, which I have never seen illustrated, is the manner in which the fourth finger of the right hand quits the stick when the point of the bow is being used. Some amateurs have but a confused idea of what this "quitting the stick" means. I noticed one lately performing in an amateur orchestra who deliberately *lifted* the little finger, stuck it right up in the air, as often as he could remember to do so. Now, the little finger leaves the stick simply because at that position of the bow it is too short to reach it. If it be kept on the stick, the bow must certainly be either drawn round the body, and so describe a curve in crossing, or, what is worse, be turned over on the string when nearing the point, so that the stick inclines towards the player instead of from him. Diagram I., showing the position of the right arm and wrist when using the point of the bow, shows the only quitting of the stick by the fourth finger which is necessary or allowable, and without which the afore-mentioned evil results would certainly appear. This diagram gives the exact lie of bow, hand, fingers, and arm when beginning an upward stroke of the bow. The hair is resting on the two middle strings, and the elevation of the arm, therefore, correct for these. For the first string the arm would be depressed a little, for the fourth elevated; but the lie of fingers and wrist would be the same.

By comparing Diagram II., showing the position of the fingers when the heel of the bow is being used, with that given by Spohr in his great work (Fig. I., plate 3), the force of my remark at page 45, fifteenth line from the top, will be apparent. To get a proper view of the face, the photographer had to raise his camera a little higher than for the first; and at that line the hair of the bow, the stick being properly inclined from the performer, is almost invisible. Spohr's diagram shows the stick perpendicular, the hair consequently lying flat on the string, and a visible space between. The same diagram, and also his Fig. IV., shows the little finger drooping *over* the stick of the bow, which is most certainly and fatally wrong, as it would be quite impossible for the finger in such a position to act as the sole balancing member. Diagram II. at the beginning of this book, and that at the top of page 44, show the proper position of the fourth finger. As the stick is *always* inclined from the performer it follows that the little finger, far from drooping over the front, touches the stick with its point rather behind than on the exact top of the stick. A bow which I have used constantly for seventeen years now shows quite a hollow in the hard Brazil wood at the spot where this touching with the point of the little finger has so often taken place.

THE VIOLIN ALONE TO BE STUDIED.

The violin is a jealous instrument, and will suffer no rival. If you give it a divided love it will resent the insult by giving you a half-hearted obedience. Those who play piano-forte and violin, with perhaps the violoncello, cornet, and flute thrown in, seldom make great attainments in either, and always play the violin roughly. Let the student understand that clearly from the first, and he will be saved from deep disappointment. If he would excel, if he would do justice to himself and the noble instrument he has chosen, he must never do more than "touch" another instrument. "What!" cries some affrighted father or mother, "would you have us bring up a girl to play the violin alone, and not give her the piano-forte as well?" Even so, sir or madam, absolute homage to the king of instruments, or none: there is no alternative. In these days, when cramming is the fashionable craze, and every young girl has to struggle through a pile of studies the very naming of which might rob a Socrates of reason, to meet with a little ignorance, if only of piano-playing, would be positively refreshing.

THE VIOLIN AS A VOICE-TRAINER.

Besides the ordinary purposes of solo and orchestral playing in which the violin shines pre-eminent I may mention another for which it seems highly suitable, leading and training young voices. It is now some years since my friend, Mr. James T. Sharpe, singing master of the Edinburgh Board Schools, tried the violin in this way as an experiment; and on inquiry I learn that it has been a singular success, the children taking their daily drilling, led by the violin, not as school drudgery, but as a pleasure, looked forward to with eagerness, and gone through with zest and intelligence. The high state of efficiency in music and singing shown by the schools under Mr. Sharpe, as attested by the government inspector's report, I take to be as much a tribute to the violin as to that gentleman's undoubted ability as a teacher. The violin is a peculiarly *human* instrument; and I have often noticed that singers with a poor or undeveloped "ear" can catch the notes from the violin, when piano or even voice have been tried in vain.

EXCEPTIONAL FINGERING.

When the notes of an imperfect fifth have to be fingered rapidly on different strings it must be done by playing the second note with a different finger from that used for the first: thus,—

No. 1. No. 2.

This interval, however, is often played best by "stretching" for the upper note, and keeping both on one string, as in Example 2. In such cases the first finger must be kept firmly on the string during the stretching.

When the notes of a perfect fifth have to be fingered rapidly on two different strings, as in many strathspeys, it is usual to put the finger firmly down fairly between both strings, so as to stop both, and so save lifting. Sometimes the finger may be pressed off the one string on to the other without rasing; but generally it is safer to finger them as indicated below. These two rules apply also to the playing of these intervals as chords.

No. 3. No. 4.

The playing of fifths thus in chords all over the finger-board is not only an excellent study, and good for developing a new violin, but it is, if there be no mechanical defect in the violin, a crucial test for the balance of the strings. If any string should be too thin or thick in proportion to the others, or if any two strings should have their thin ends turned in opposite directions, it will be literally impossible to get a pure, true fifth thus.

COMMON FAULTS IN FINGERING.

Never raise the fingers higher than is necessary to free the string,

Do not raise at all the fingers which have been used on a string until actually compelled to do so.

In playing upon the sharp keys, such as D, A, or E, while on the first position, it is a common fault to play the sharpened note, fingered with the third finger, and especially the C sharp on the fourth string, a slight degree flat. This fault is most common when the sharp note is used as part of a chord. An effort should be made rather to finger these notes sharp than flat, the result of which effort will generally be that they will be played perfectly in tune. In like manner it is common for even good players to finger F♯, first string; B♭, second string; E♭, third string; and A♭, fourth string (playing on the first position), a slight degree sharp.

Early attention to these probable errors and the "ear" of the student will effectually prevent a habit which only too easily becomes chronic.

PERFORMING IN PUBLIC.

When about to play in public keep your violin in your hand, with your fingers working on the strings on all the positions, with or without the bow, for some time before you have to appear on the platform. The object is to warm the strings, and accustom them to a heightened temperature and tension; and the result will be that the violin will be less apt to go seriously out of tune during the performance. The atmosphere on the platform of a crowded public hall, though that part should be only two feet off the floor, is always many degrees warmer and more humid than that on the level.

TO TUNE QUIETLY.

Avoid the fidgety habit of scraping and tuning in public. Keep the fingers off the strings, except when using the violin, when once fairly on the platform. If you *know* that not one but all of the strings of your instrument have altered seriously with the raised temperature, tune quietly thus: Tune the A by resting the head of the violin on the knee, turning the peg with the right hand, and twitching softly with the thumb of the *left hand* till it is in tune. Many seem to be ignorant of the fact that they have a thumb on the left hand while tuning thus, and first turn the peg and then twitch the string with the same thumb which has been employed to move the peg. The A being tuned to pitch, tune the E to it in the same manner; then raise the violin into position as for ordinary tuning, turn the violin-bow upside down on the string, having the forefinger of the right hand hooked round the stick near the nut; and then, while turning the peg, *beat* lightly and rapidly the two strings to be tuned (first A and D, then D and G) with the point of the stick of the bow. This beating with the stick, though producing a faint and fairy-like sound, gives the fifth perfectly well to a good ear, and is, if not inaudible to the audience, at least faint enough to cause no annoyance. The strings may then be tested by sounding the harmonics in the centre of the string, one after another, which testing may be repeated at any time when there is a doubt whether the violin be in tune. The insufferable tune, tuning so inseparable from the performances of amateur orchestras, is nothing but an unchecked and pernicious habit. Let your fiddles alone; let them have some peace, and it is wonderful how well they will adjust themselves to altered circumstances. If they sink in pitch, the probability is that they will *all sink* pretty much alike, in which case performers on the wind instruments, if they have not the sense to flatten, will get all the blame for "playing sharp."

TO TUNE HURRIEDLY.

Occasionally, when playing in public, the performer cannot adjust a string exactly to pitch by moving the peg, which either sharpens or flattens the note too much; or, again, he may not have time to touch the peg, and then sound the strings in the ordinary manner, and yet be painfully conscious that one of his strings is not in tune. In these circumstances (1) a string slightly sharp may be flattened by tugging it more or less strongly between the bridge and the nut; (2) a string slightly flat may be raised in pitch by pressing down with the point of the finger that part of the string which lies within the box of the scroll between the nut and the peg.

TAKING DIFFICULT SHIFTS.

When compelled, for the sake of a good shake or a rapid fingering, to play a particular passage on a position difficult of attack,—such as the second or fourth,—get into the position, if possible, some bars in advance of the passage which demands the change, especially at some quiet or slow notes where you can *hear* that you are playing in tune, and that you are therefore on the exact position. Example: the conclusion of La Gazza Ladra Overture, get on to the fourth position somewhere between the seventeenth and fourteenth bars from the end.

For attacking the second position safely, see page 57. To attack the fourth position with accuracy, sweeping up from the first, keep the first or any other handy finger firmly on the string, and slide the hand as close up as it will go against the ribs of the violin, without bringing the thumb in below the neck. If this be done carefully you will generally find the fingers exactly on the fourth position.

When compelled to make a sudden jump from a high note to a low note, or a succession of such jumps, whether the high notes be accented or not, *play the high note with an up bow.* When jumping from a low note to a high one, *play the low note with a down bow*: thus,—

No. 5. No. 6.

Do not adhere slavishly to the rule for giving a down bow to the accented note, more especially in slow movements, but accustom yourself to play with comfort either way. Exercises 6, 7, 10, and 12 in Kreutzer's "Studies," and 46 and 47 in Spohr, are designed for giving this power; and there are several in Loder adapted to the same purpose. In playing concerted music, however, the conductor will generally superintend the conduct of the bows, and see that they are uniform, especially in passages of a bold or marked character, so that the performance may be a picture to the eye as well as to the ear.

THE ACQUISITION OF TONE.

Tone is to be developed and acquired by (1) a swift, light, and smooth carriage of the bow across the strings to its entire length (see page 47, ninth line from the bottom); by (2) studying from the first to acquire sweetness and smoothness rather than rapidity of execution; by (3) strictly following the advice of Tartini (page 44) regarding the first contact of the bow; and, (4) most important, by guarding against any roughness at that critical moment when the bow is reversed, to move up or down. Playing fast or slow, that is the point to be watched. Playing fast, say a page of semiquavers marked *allegro*, such as those exercises alluded to at page 52, every note should be round and smooth, or, if marked *staccato*, should be picked out clean and neat, as if a rest were inserted between the notes, but never with the slightest scuffling, scratchiness, or even looseness of tone. This result, where there is much crossing from one string to another, can be brought about only by using the upper third part of the bow, from that division to the extreme point, and by strict attention to the flexibility and carriage of the wrist of the right hand and the balance of the bow. Where there is *not* much crossing from one string to another, and a specially powerful tone is desired, the middle third part or even the heel of the bow may be used, as for example in the *ff* passages in the violin part of "For unto us a Son is born;" but to use the heel is only allowable with the most experienced players. In long notes tone is gained by allowing the stick of the bow to rise slightly by diminishing the pressure of the first finger on the stick at the moment of reversing. Too much attention is paid by most teachers to the left hand and its work; and I have met dozens of young pupils able to play far into Loder or Spohr, who, nevertheless, could not play eight different notes rapidly in a neat and clean manner. Execution and fingering with the left hand should never be got at the expense of tone. It is true, as indicated on page 83, that a really fine tone only comes to the violinist after many years' practice, but to some it never comes at all; and with all I feel assured it will come the sooner from that perfection of playing being put before the pupil from the first as *the* goal to be striven for. All distinguished performers are judged in comparison with each other almost solely by the tone they produce, the mere execution being generally accorded a secondary place in legitimate criticism as a mechanism of detail attainable by all willing to work hard.

LEGATO PLAYING.

In *legato* passages keep as much as possible on one string, though this should necessitate a deal of shifting. With novices these passages must all be studied separately, and several different fingerings tried before the most effective is decided upon. Experienced players know almost at a glance how alone they can be properly executed. The very shifting and sliding about, if properly done, aids the *legato* effect, and helps the violin to sing. In these passages the hair of the bow must never leave the string, and the reversing must be so artistically managed, according to the method just explained, as to cause no perceptible break to the ear.

"STACCATO."—ITS DIFFERENT MEANINGS.

It seems time that a classified distinction were made in the different kinds of *staccato* playing, and the method of marking and playing these. At page 74 I have noted three styles of playing these when a number are linked to one bow. The classification to which I now allude is chiefly for those styles which receive a separate bow to each note. There are two modes of marking staccato; namely, with a number of dots, or with points or dashes over the notes, as in the examples given on the next page.

Many composers seem to use these markings indiscriminately. In No. 7, which I may here name the *stopped staccato*, the notes in the second bar are played by stopping the bow, and allowing the hair to rest on the string, and check the vibrations for a mere second of time between each note. There is no "biting out" of the notes,—merely the neat picking out and resting of the hair; and this style cannot be used for any rapid movement. No. 9, which is suitable for the most rapid movement, I may name the *rounded staccato*. The notes are played only a little sharper than if they were not marked with dots. Neat and clean would express the treatment of these notes better than staccato, and the hair of the bow does not entirely leave the string between each note. It is played an inch or two nearer the heel of the bow than the middle, and thus gets a spring from the extra weight of the stick above the string, which raises part of the hair from the string between each note. To Example No. 8 the term *staccato leggiero* may legitimately be applied, and I would suggest that it be applied to no other style of *staccato.* This style, which is noticed at the bottom of page 55, is played at the middle of the bow, or an inch or so above the middle, and the bow bounds from the string between every note. A number of these *staccato leggiero* notes (which, I think, ought always to be marked with the points or dashes; thus, ' ' ' ') are sometimes linked to one bow, as in No. 10.

No. 7. No. 8.

Andante.

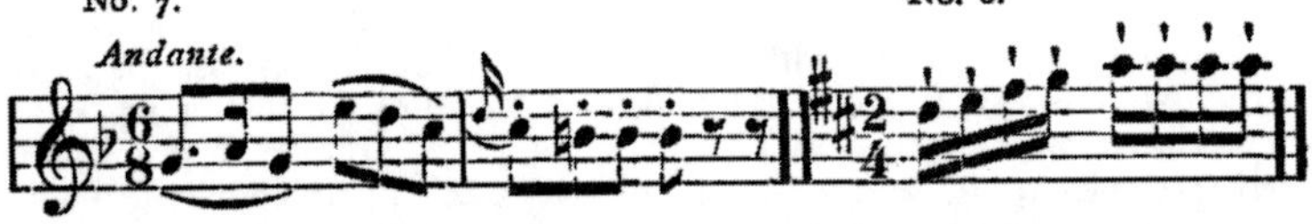

No. 9. No. 10.

And the bow still bounds on the string, and entirely quits it between each note, which forms a marked distinction between this bowing and the *staccato bow* noticed at page 76. This last-mentioned *staccato leggiero* is very neat and effective in *arpeggios,* and also in short phrases, alternately slurred and detached.

"BEATING" TIME.

Whether taking part in concerted music, or studying alone, the player must *never* audibly beat the floor with his foot. It is surprising how many get into this habit, as unnecessary as it is irritating. I have more than once had to stand on the right foot of a new pupil, during the performance of his study, to keep it from moving, after finding repeated checkings useless. Not long ago I was playing beside a soloist already mentioned in these pages, who was leading with me the first violins at an orchestral concert; and he beat the floor with his foot so persistently, that at length I was compelled to silently rebuke him by looking straight and fiercely down at the offending foot. He troubled me no more during the evening with his beating. I must say, however, that players of wind instruments more frequently transgress in this respect than violinists; and it is not an exaggeration to say that there is at this moment scarcely one amateur brass band in existence which has not one or two of these vulgar "stampers" among its members. The counting, as described at page 86, must be strictly *mental,* without any moving of the lips, or, what is worse, any *sotto voce* whispering or muttering of the numbers. I once played with an amateur, who appeared a kind of demon planted behind me for the sole purpose of teaching me patience. No matter how soft the music, or how long the rest, there was that gentleman earnestly and fiercely hissing out his "one — two — three — four" in a cold whisper distinctly audible several rows off.

LEFT-HANDED.

The left-handed student who wishes to play the violin must have the instrument altered to suit the defect in his frame. The finger-board must be raised at the front instead of the back, and the bass bar removed to the opposite side; the bridge being depressed at the left-hand side to suit the depressed finger-board. I never met any distinguished left-handed player, though Mr. Charles Reade, who is an enthusiast in left hands as well in violins, may be better informed.

THE POSITION OF THE LEFT HAND.

I would again impress upon all the necessity of attending strictly to the direction given at the foot of page 37, regarding the position of the first finger as it rests against the side of the neck of the violin. The first finger should always be kept low, — never a hair's breadth above the crease alluded to; and to insure this the point of the first finger ought to be kept as much and as often as possible pressed down on the string. I lately met a player who allowed the crease to rise a little above the edge of the finger-board, and who consequently was playing with the ball of the finger pressed against the round neck, — a most painful position when long continued. To play with the ball of the finger thus pressed against the neck of the violin, instead of sunk below, is, if any thing, worse than having the neck sunk in the fork of the thumb, as described at page 38; for it induces the overtasked bone to throw out a thick cartilage for its protection, which in time becomes an ugly protuberance, as sensitive to pressure as a bunion. If the player therefore should find that such a protuberance is being formed on his hand, he may decide at once that he is holding the first finger too high. The same gentleman innocently complained to me of his inability to finger deftly the upper notes on the fifth position, and was quite surprised when I pointed out the raising of the first finger above its proper position as the cause. He had been induced to take this position with the idea of fingering the notes with the extreme point of the first finger, — actually on the nail, — instead of inclining towards the inside of the point, as is necessary with this particular finger. A difficulty in fingering notes with the third and fourth fingers is the least of the evils springing from this false position of the hand; the most serious being that it is extremely difficult to play always in tune, especially when playing chords or doubling octaves. *Keep down the first finger* on the string on all positions, however high, and it is almost impossible to hold the hand wrong.

THE DRIVEN NOTE IN STRATHSPEYS.

As there is a danger of misunderstanding the example given at the top of page 66, I may here explain that the driven note there given, the first note in the first complete bar, or any other similar driven note, can be caught off an up bow just as effectively as off a down bow. All depends on the exigencies of the particular tune being played. Only, whether up or down, the note must be caught off that which precedes it, and with a sharp jerk of the bow in the same direction; the note following the driven one getting a new bow to itself, and, possibly, to some which may follow it. That is the rule. Exceptions are such phrases as the second last bar of "Clachnacudin Strathspey," in which a distinct bow must be given to each note, care being taken not to begin the series near the heel, lest the bow should be too soon expended. I have already said that the bowing of the driven note is only another form of the ordinary bowing of a dotted note; and I here give an exercise,

which I have devised to demonstrate that fact, and at the same time show that the driven note may be caught off an up bow, though it is more common to jerk it at the tip of the bow off a down stroke. I need scarcely add, that, when the student can play even this short example correctly, he can play any number of such bowings as they occur in strathspeys of all kinds.

In playing the example the bow must be swept its whole length across the string firmly and swiftly, and the short note jerked off in the same direction at its extremity, heel, or point.

SIDE SLIPPING.—AN ADAPTED FIDDLE-HOLDER.

Nearly every violinist has been at times troubled with side slipping, necessitating a constant watchfulness and firm gripping of the chin during the entire performance. It is peculiarly irritating during the performance of a solo, in which the most perfect repose of the violin is called for. I believe I have now discovered a perfect remedy for the annoyance, and one within the reach of every player.

In looking at a violin-holder submitted to me lately, it struck me that it might be altered judiciously. This holder has always seemed to me defective in shape, necessitating the chin being placed *on* the holder, and the violin being held too far out from the performer. The further out the violin is held, the more difficult is it to keep the bow parallel with the bridge when using the point. I therefore, instead of using it in its oval shape, cut the rounded side completely away, thus reducing it to a neat rim, three-quarters of an inch in width. The inner side I sloped off with a file, like the design at page 33, and the holder was perfect. I could now pass my chin completely over the holder, and let it rest on the breast of the violin, the lightest grip sufficing to retain and steady the instrument. The holder thus adapted has several advantages over the ordinary narrow-rim holder. It is (1) higher and broader, and allows a deeper grip of the violin, and consequently more command with the bow; (2) it touches the instrument only at its outer edge, and consequently does not mute the tone of the violin; and it is delightfully comfortable, and effectually prevents side slipping, as well as forward slipping, of the violin. I have shown the adapted holder to several using the Joachim in its ordinary shape, and they have at once decided to have their own altered to this form.

VIOLIN-CLEANER.

It is well to keep the varnish of the violin clean and bright. On no account should an unsightly powdering of rosin be allowed to accumulate on the breast in front of the bridge, as that tends to clog the vibrations, and attracts damp. Through the kindness of Dr. Dickson I am enabled to give the receipt for his excellent violin-cleaning mixture:—

Fine raw linseed oil, 7 parts.
Oil of turpentine, 1 part.
Water, 4 parts.

Shake the bottle, pour some of the mixture on a cloth, and rub rapidly over the violin; then wipe off every particle, and rub up with another soft cloth.

FINE ROSIN FOR SOLO PLAYING.

For ordinary orchestral use common rosin far excels that sold in prepared cakes under all kinds of euphonious names; but for solo and all fine playing the following preparations, used by German soloists, and by them kept as secret as possible, will be found unapproachable by any that can be bought. The tone it produces is crisp, clean, and artistic; and using it on good, clean hair, a harsh or whizzing note is almost an impossibility. The recipe, which, so far as I know, has never before been made public, is certainly as extraordinary as it is simple; but I can testify most emphatically to its value.

Take two tablespoonfuls of rosin, selected, clear and pale in color, and pounded fine, and place it in a clean, new tin dish (earthenware will not do). Place the tin dish in a hot oven till the rosin melts; then stir it slowly three times with a common tallow "dip" candle. Let the rosin remain in the oven for a quarter of an hour, then pour it into a box, and keep stirring with a clean stick till it begins to "set." Ointment-boxes of wood chip, bought new from the druggist's, are very suitable, as they can be cut down as the rosin is used, the lid still fitting and keeping all tidy and clean.

CONCLUSION.

In finishing what I trust will be a useful addition to this work I wish to thank the many correspondents who have addressed me for their warm expressions of pleasure and satisfaction. Especially gratifying has it been to me to find among these correspondents teachers of experience writing to me in approval, and ordering copies expressly for their pupils. In penning and issuing this treatise I was a little doubtful of being misunderstood by teachers, and possibly of being accused of trenching upon their ground. That I have not been so misunderstood is only another proof of what I have said on 89, and encourages me to hope that, in creating an enthusiasm for this matchless instrument, I may be increasing, rather than diminishing, the number requiring good tuition from competent teachers; and that in the words of one kind critic the work "will enable them to teach more intelligently, while pupils will be more apt to receive such instruction, and to profit largely by it."

THE VIOLIN: HOW TO MASTER IT.

BY A PROFESSIONAL PLAYER.

OPINIONS OF THE PRESS.

"To find a really plain and practical guide to any branch of study is quite a rarity; for generally so-called guides are so filled with technical terms and ambiguous phrases as often to puzzle the most skilful expert. In the present work, however, the author places his instruction in such a way before his pupil as to render his meaning clear at a first glance. To all who love the violin, but do not know how to master it, we would say, procure this little book, and many of the difficulties will be instantly smoothed away."—*The World.*

"The writer of this book has accomplished a task of no common difficulty with uncommon ability and singular success. The difficulty is, that of giving such verbal instruction in an art as the student without example can clearly understand, and put to practical use with certainty and safety. This the author does from an evidently thorough knowledge of the subject, a capability of placing himself on the same level with his pupil, and from an unbounded enthusiasm for the instrument whose power he is describing. He leaves no point untouched. One feels on reading the book as if being talked to by a teacher whose sympathies are keenly alive to every possible doubt and difficulty, as if a violin and bow were being put into his hand, and his every act therewith under strictest surveillance. It is a book that ought to be, and indeed will be, in the hands of every one who either plays or means to play the violin, being the most comprehensive, the most precise, most perspicuous, and withal the least costly of any book of instruction in violin-playing ever issued."—*Advertiser.*

"An excellent manual. Here, too, are full details of the playing of Scotch dance music, so puzzling to players. The professional violinist might learn something from its pages, while there can be no question that, as regards the amateur, this book supplies a want. The instruction even of a good teacher requires to be supplemented by more information to be available at all times. This the book furnishes, and that excellently. The work deserves to be known by all players. Teachers will do well to put it in the hands of their pupils. It will enable them to teach more intelligently, while the pupils will be more apt to receive instruction, and to profit largely by it."—*Weekly Journal.*

"A very handy, sensible book, furnishing much valuable information and a great deal of interesting talk about the 'king of the orchestra.' The observations on bowing are most clear, and to the point. 'Harmonic playing,' too, is dealt with with admirable lucidity. The choice and preservation of an instrument, and many other topics connected with its mastery and care, are equally well handled."—*Musical Standard.*

"A better mentor than this book a learner of the violin could not have, and even those regarded as proficient cannot fail to be benefited by a study of its pages. The book is admirably illustrated, and is sure to meet with general approval."—*Musical Gazette.*

"It is violin-teaching popularized by one whom we know to be a proficient and skilful player, and whose understanding of the instrument is as nearly as possible perfect. To this he adds a style of lucid exposition which enables him to make every line and sentence understood. The work is thorough in treatment and exhaustive in scope, and should be in the hands of all who desire to become really proficient players."—*Evening Telegraph.*

"This is really a pleasant, profitable, and useful manual of how to play the violin. The writer is a professional, and takes the pupil into his confidence, and makes a difficult study at once interesting and entertaining. We commend the hearty manner in which the varied and useful information is imparted, and wish the treatise a wide circulation." — *Art Journal.*

"To the violinist this work on his or her favorite instrument cannot fail to be acceptable; and as a handbook for the novice it will be equally useful, teaching him what to study and what to avoid, thus marking out many rocks and shoals on which he may become a hopeless and disgusted shipwreck. The author has arranged his matter in a candid and progressive manner, giving sufficient instruction on the various subjects connected with violin-playing." — *Graphic.*

"This is a text-book for the violin which from begining to end shows its author to be thoroughly in sympathy with the task he has undertaken, and well acquainted with the instrument about which he writes. With considerable skill and minuteness he has produced an admirable guide. Directions what to imitate and what to avoid are given with sufficient clearness to prove a boon to those struggling to master the instrument. Illustrations are supplied where necessary; and the book is written by one who, while withholding his name, wishes to save others 'years of weary struggling, and blind groping, and retracing of steps and unlearning of evil habits of style.'" — *Daily Review.*

"A complete treatise on the violin. The author being himself a professional player, who has had a long experience, is a most competent instructor. Premising that self-tuition is perfectly possible he leads the student step by step from things comparatively simple to things difficult and intricate, the result being that the tyro who pays strict attention to the instructions and practises patiently and diligently will very soon acquire a mastery over his instrument, and be able to play high-class music. Let the tyro submit himself implicitly to its guidance, and he can scarcely fail to become a proficient violinist." — *People's Journal.*

"The popular style in which this treatise is written should strongly recommend it to students. The very questions they constantly desire to ask are here more plainly answered than in works of the greatest authorities upon the instrument. There are good observations on the choice of an instrument; salutary cautions against the tricks of unscrupulous manufacturers; many practical hints respecting holding, stringing, tuning, bowing, etc.; and some very useful directions as to the course of study to be pursued, the standard books being recommended in systematic order. Many students will thank the author for his labors on their behalf." — *Musical Times.*

"This is what it professes to be, — a practical exposition of the difficulties of the violin, and how to master these; and the student cannot fail to find valuable instruction in the clear and concise explanations." — *The Weekly Chronicle.*

"This book on the violin is full of shrewd, practical advice and instruction, and forms a very valuable supplement to the regular manuals, such as Spohr's and Loder's. The author has contrived to make his work readable and interesting as well as instructive. He treats his theme with real enthusiasm." — *The Republican.*

"It is wonderful, well-packed, comprehensive, and thoroughly practical." — *Critic.*

WHITE'S EDITION
—OF—
CELEBRATED INSTRUMENTAL WORKS.

VIOLIN SOLO.

1311. **Dancla, Charles.** School of Mechanism for the Violin, being Fifty Daily Exercises, composed and designed for movement of the left hand, and to give to the fingers independence, equality of strength and flexibility. The value of such a work, to be used in conjunction with the regular instruction book, will at once be apparent to all teachers and students, while professional players will find it very helpful in remedying defects of early training.
Price, complete, net, . $0.60

1074. **Kreutzer.** Forty Celebrated Studies for the Violin. F. David's edition.
This is one of the finest editions of these Celebrated Studies, printed on the best of paper, from large size music plates, and is similar and in every way equal to the two dollar and fifty cent edition.
Price, complete, net, . $1.00

1081. **DeBeriot, Chas.** Violinist's First Guide, consisting of elementary studies for the violin.
The finest set of elementary violin studies in existence. Indispensable to all teachers and students.
Price, complete, net, . $1.00

1323. **Alard, D.** Twenty-four Italian Melodies for *Violin Solo*, from the favorite Operas of Bellini, Donizetti, Mercadante, Rossini, and Verdi, arranged by D. Alard, Professor of the Violin at the Conservatory of Music, Paris. These solos are adapted to the use of amateurs of good attainments as well as professional musicians, and will be found quite helpful in cultivating a taste for music of a high order.
Price of the 24 Melodies, net, $0.75

TWO VIOLINS.

1315. **DeBeriot, Chas.** Twelve Easy and Progressive Duets for Two Violins. DeBeriot's works have long held a high place in the esteem of violin students. These duets combine many of his more prominent characteristics, are quite easy at commencement, and very progressive: and on this account of great value to teachers and students of the violin.
Price of the twelve duets for two violins, complete, net, . $0.75

1052. **Alard, D.** Conservatoire Studies for the violin. A collection of easy and progressive studies for the violin, arranged in the form of duets. By D. Alard, Professor of the Violin at the Conservatoire of Music, Paris.
The above celebrated studies are a standard work in the Conservatoire of Music, Paris, and are just the thing needed by all teachers of the violin.
Price, complete, net, . $0.75

1069. **Pleyel.** Six Celebrated Easy Duets for Two Violins. Each part separate.
These celebrated duets have a world-wide reputation, and should be in the possession of every teacher and beginner.
Price, 2 parts complete, net, $0.50

1318b. **Wichtl, G.** Operatic Bouquet, consisting of Themes of the favorite Standard Operas, arranged by G. Wichtl, for two violins, in the first position — instructive, easy and brilliant. The Themes are from "Il Trovatore" (Verdi), "La Traviata" (Verdi), "The Merry Wives of Windsor" (Nicolai), "Orphee aux Enfers" (Offenbach), "Ernani" (Verdi), "Faust" (Gounod), "The Star of the North" (Meyerbeer), "Rigoletto" (Verdi), "The Prophet" (Meyerbeer), "The Jewess" (Halevy), "The Sicilian Vespers" (Verdi), and "The Bohemian Girl" (Balfe).
This arrangement is admirably adapted for the use of amateurs and players of fair acquirements.
Price of the 12 pieces, complete, for two violins, . . . $0.75

1322. **Kayser, H. E.** "Recollections of the Operas," for Two Violins. This splendid collection of gems consists of themes from the favorite operas, arranged for Two Violins, selections being made from the most popular works of Auber, Bellini, Donizetti, Meyerbeer, Mozart, Rossini, Verdi, Weber, etc., and adapted in an easy and agreeable style, by H. E. Kayser.
Price of the entire work, arranged for Two Violins, . . $1.00

The above editions are the finest ever offered the American public, equal, if not superior to the very best German editions; printed on extra heavy plate paper, from beautifully engraved, large size music plates, and sold at marvellously low prices, which places them within the reach of all.

INSTRUMENTAL WORKS—Continued.

VIOLIN AND PIANO.

1310. **DeBeriot, Chas.** Twelve Italian Melodies, for the Violin, with accompaniment for Piano. Arranged by Chas. DeBeriot.

These are issued in the best style possible, and adapted for use in public or in the home circle.

CONTENTS.

Non giova il Sospirar,
Vanne al mio bene,
Al dolce-guidami,
A torto ti lagno,
E vezzose si la roso,
La verginella,
Mille Sospiri e lagrime,
Deh! non voler constingere,
Come l'aurette placide,
Stanca di pascolar,
Quel Suono,
Prendimi teco.

Price for the twelve pieces, arranged for Violin and Piano, complete, net, . . $1.00

1309. **Thirlwall, J.W.** Favorite Airs, arranged with variations for the Violin, with Piano Accompaniment, consisting of favorite English, Scotch, Irish and Welsh Airs.

This work contains sixty elegantly engraved, large sized music pages, and is published in the very best style. Each part separate.

CONTENTS.

English Air,
Scotch Air (Annie Laurie),
Ye Banks and Braes,
Welsh Air (Poor Mary Ann),
Irish Air (Sprig of Shillalah),
Old English Song (Malibran's Favorite),
Northumbrian Air (Weel may the Keel Row).

Price, Violin and Piano parts complete, net, ... $1.50

1126. **Dancla, Chas.** Twelve easy Fantasies on Celebrated Melodies, for the Violin, with accompaniment for Piano. Each part separate.

CONTENTS.

Norma Semiramide Elisire,
Der Freischutz,
Redowa de Wallerstein,
Donna del Lago. Air Suisse,
Hymne Autrichien. Don Juan,
Derniere Pensee de Weber,
Cenerentola,
Fleuve du Tage. La Romanesca,
Les Puritains,
Les Noces de Figaro. Crociato,
Le Cordes Alpes. Valse du Freischutz,
Plaisir d'Amour.

Price of the above twelve pieces, arranged for Violin and Piano, complete, net, . . . $1.00

1312. **Dancla, Chas.** Eight very pleasing Melodies for the Violin, with an accompaniment for the Piano. Each part separate. Prof. Dancla's reputation as an instructor is abundantly justified by his compositions designed for pupils who have reached various degrees of proficiency.

CONTENTS.

Valse,
Petit Fragment de Sonate,
Petit Air de Ballet,
Melodie Elegante,
Petite Etude Chantante,
Petite Bolero,
Berceuse,
Petite Gavotte.

Price of the above eight pieces (Violin and Piano complete), net, ... $1.00

1314. **DeBeriot, Chas.** "The Three Bouquets," being three brilliant Fantasias, for the Violin, with Piano accompaniment, written in DeBeriot's best vein, and sure of a warm welcome from instructors and pupils. Not difficult.

Price of the three pieces with Piano accompaniment. Each part separate. Net. . $0.75

1316. **Dancla, Chas.** Twenty-four easy, useful and agreeable Melodies for Violin, with Piano accompaniment, in all the keys. Each melody is preceded by the scale in major or minor, and the common chord in successive tones. This group of melodies is peculiarly adapted for the advancement of pupils to the highest grades of studies

Price, Violin and Piano complete, net, ... $2.00

1319. **Wohlfahrt, Franz.** Fourteen easy and instructive fantasias for violin and piano, by Franz Wohlfahrt, as follows: "My Heart, Why so Sad," 'Green Meadows," "In the Cool Ground," "Drink to Our Health," "Dear Home of My Beloved," "On Swift Wings," "Tyrolean Song," "Ring the Glasses," "Gently through My Bosom," "A Hunter's Song," "A Bridal Wreath We Twine for Thee," "See the Three Steeds," "I and Doctor Blue Beard," and "Thou Art in My Heart."

Amateurs and violin students will find these fantasias very useful and pleasing, either as pastimes or for practice. The music is all of an entertaining and instructive character.

Price, net, . . . $1.00

1318c. **Wichtl, G.** Operatic Bouquet, consisting of Themes of the favorite Standard Operas, arranged by G. Wichtl for violin and piano, in the first position — instructive, easy, and brilliant. The Themes are from "Il Trovatore" (Verdi), "La Traviata" (Verdi), "The Merry Wives of Windsor" (Nicolai), "Orphee aux Enfers" (Offenbach), "Ernani" (Verdi), "Faust" (Gounod), "The Star of the North" (Meyerbeer), "Rigoletto" (Verdi), "The Prophet" (Meyerbeer), "The Jewess" (Halevy), "The Sicilian Vespers" (Verdi), and "The Bohemian Girl" (Balfe).

This arrangement is admirably adapted for the use of amateurs and players of fair acquirements.

Price of the 12 pieces complete, for violin and piano, . . $1.00

TWO VIOLINS AND PIANO.

1129. **Dancla Chas.** Six Easy Melodic Pieces, For Two Violins, with Piano Accompaniment. Each part separate.

CONTENTS.

Andante Cantabile,
Valse,
Andante Cantabile,
Barcarolle,
Nocturne,
Priere.

Price, Two Violins and Piano, complete, net, . . $1.00

1318d. **Wichtl, G.** Operatic Bouquet, consisting of Themes of the favorite Standard Operas, arranged by G. Wichtl for two violins and piano, in the first position — instructive, easy and brilliant. The Themes are from "Il Trovatore" (Verdi), "La Traviata" (Verdi), "The Merry Wives of Windsor" (Nicolai), "Orphee aux Enfers" (Offenbach), "Ernani" (Verdi), "Faust" (Gounod), "The Star of the North" (Meyerbeer), "Rigoletto" (Verdi), "The Prophet" (Meyerbeer), "The Jewess" (Halevy), "The Sicilian Vespers" (Verdi), and "The Bohemian Girl" (Balfe).

This arrangement is admirably adapted for the use of amateurs and players of fair acquirements.

Price of the 12 pieces complete, for two violins and piano, $1.25

1313. **Dancla, Chas.** "Three Petite Symphonies," for two Violins, with piano accompaniment. These exquisite gems are published in the very best style, and will constitute a most welcome addition to a violinist's collection.

Petite Symphonie No. 1.
Petite Symphonie No. 2.
Petite Symphonie No. 3.

Price of the three Petite Symphonies for two Violins, with Piano Accompaniment, complete, net, $1.00

CORNET AND PIANO.

1320. **Molique, B.** Six lovely Melodies, for Cornet and Piano, designed for Amateur use in the parlor.

This addition to the collections of musicians of fair attainments will be most welcome. The titles of the "Six Melodies" are

If o'er the Boundless Sky.
Fair Annie.
When the Moon is Brightly Beaming.
Come all ye Glad and Free.
Come, Dearest, Come.
O, that my Woes were Distant.

Price of the six Melodies, arranged for Cornet and Piano, complete, net, ... $0.75

FLUTE, VIOLIN AND PIANO.

1329. **Kuffner, J.** Six Nocturnes for Flute and Violin, with Piano accompaniment. The combination of these three popular instruments is a favorite one both in amateur and professional circles, and musicians will take exquisite pleasure in the performance of these beautiful nocturnes, which afford ample opportunity for bringing out the best qualities of the instruments.

Price of the Six Nocturnes, arranged for Flute, Violin and Piano, complete, net, . $1.00